The CIA in Hollywood

The CIA in Hollywood

How the Agency Shapes
Film and Television

TRICIA JENKINS

University of Texas Press ⋀⋁ *Austin*

Library of Congress Cataloging-in-Publication Data

Jenkins, Tricia.
The CIA in Hollywood : how the agency shapes film and television /
Tricia Jenkins. — 1st ed.
       p.   cm.
Includes bibliographical references and index.
ISBN 978-0-292-75436-2
1. Spy films—United States—History and criticism.   2. United States. Central
Intelligence Agency—In motion pictures.   3. Espionage in motion pictures.
4. Motion pictures—Political aspects—United States.   5. Motion picture
industry—United States.   6. Spy television programs—United States—History
and criticism.   7. United States. Central Intelligence Agency—Influence.
I. Title.   II. Title: Central Intelligence Agency in Hollywood.
PN1995.9.S68J46   2011
791.43'651—dc23   2011027163

Contents

Acknowledgments

This book was a pleasure to research and write, largely because I got to interact with so many interesting people. These include former CIA directors of public affairs Kent Harrington and Bill Harlow; current and retired CIA employees like Paula Weiss, Paul Barry, Robert Baer, Antonio and Jonna Mendez, John Strauchs, Nicholas Dujmovic, and Peter Ernest; and several entertainment professionals, including Michael Sands, Michael Frost Beckner, Jack Myers, David Houle, Bazzel Baz, James Grady, Peter Iliff, Matt Corman, and Chris Ord. Thanks to each of you for taking the time to answer my questions. This book would not have been possible without your help.

Other people also aided my work on this book. I would specifically like to thank Matthew Alford and David Robb, who shared their resources, knowledge, and contacts with me. Nicholas Taylor, Joan McGettigan, Joel Timmer, Benjamin Martinez, Matthew Alford, and David Culbert also read some or all of this book and provided me with useful feedback as I went through the revision process. I would also like to express my appreciation to Sacred Heart University, which provided me with funds to travel to the CIA headquarters to interview Paul Barry in 2008, and to Texas Christian University for giving me a Junior Faculty Research Grant to complete this project.

Most important, I would like to thank my husband, Nathanael O'Reilly, for his support and encouragement. He read every word of this book, often more than once, and offered several critical and editorial insights. He also watched more spy films and television series than any one man could reasonably expect to enjoy just so we could talk knowledgably about this topic together. Thank you.

Introduction

Agencies of the U.S. government have long employed entertainment liaison officers to improve their public image in the mass media. For instance, the Federal Bureau of Investigation established an office in the 1930s to bolster its image in radio programs, films, and television shows, including *G-Men* (1935), *The FBI Story* (1959), and *The F.B.I.* (1965–1974). In 1947, the Department of Defense followed suit, and now the army, the navy, the air force, the marine corps, the coast guard, the Department of Homeland Security, and the Secret Service all have motion picture and television offices or official assistants to the media on their payroll. Even government centers are currently working with Tinseltown, as evidenced by Hollywood, Health, and Society—a program partially funded by the Centers for Disease Control and Prevention and the National Institutes of Health to provide the entertainment industry with information on health-related story lines.

Despite the fact that it has existed since 1947, the Central Intelligence Agency was the last major government agency to establish formal relations with the motion picture industry. In fact, it did not found a basic entertainment program until the early 1990s and did not hire Chase Brandon as its first entertainment industry liaison officer until 1996. Perhaps because its efforts in film and television are relatively new, only a very small amount of scholarship has examined the CIA's collaborations, motivations, and methodologies in this field. The lack of scholarship is surprising, however, given that the Agency has already shaped the content of numerous film and television works, including *JAG* (1995–2005), *Enemy of the State* (1998), *In the Company of Spies* (1999), *The Agency* (2001–2003), *Alias* (2001–2006), *24* (2001–2010), *Bad Company* (2002), *The Sum of All Fears* (2002), *The Recruit* (2003), *Covert Affairs* (2010–), and *Argo* (in production). CIA administrators have also met with studio heads and the-atrical agents in order to influence their ideas about the Agency more broadly, and its retired officers have likewise contributed to numerous films, including *Sneakers* (1992), *Meet the Parents* (2000), *Syriana* (2005), *The Good Shepherd* (2006), *Rendition* (2007), *Charlie Wilson's War* (2007), *Salt* (2010), and *Red* (2010).

As a result, this book sets out to answer a number of important questions regarding the CIA and its involvement in Hollywood (which here is used as a shorthand term to describe both the American film and television industry). These questions include: What is the nature of the CIA's role in the motion picture industry? What texts has the CIA influenced and to what ends? What events motivated Langley (here used as short-hand for the CIA as whole) to reverse its closed-door policy regarding Hollywood in the 1990s? How does the role of the retired CIA officer in the entertainment industry differ from the role of the Agency, and why have these retirees generated so much government flak? How has film and television traditionally depicted the Agency? And what are the legal and ethical concerns that a relationship between the CIA and Hollywood present, especially in a democracy?

In order to answer these questions, this book employs a close textual analysis of several CIA-assisted texts and incorporates existing scholarship and journalism on the topic. Perhaps most significant, however, *The CIA in Hollywood* also draws from numerous interviews I conducted with the CIA's public affairs staff, operations officers, and historians, as well as with Hollywood technical consultants, producers, and screenwriters who have worked with the Agency over the years. These interviews provide greater insight into the nature of CIA-assisted texts and an additional behind-the-scenes, production economy perspective.

This book is important because very few people know that the CIA has been actively engaged in shaping the content of film and television, and they fail to understand how or even why the Agency has become more formally involved with this sector in the last fifteen years. Additionally, as Matthew Alford and Robbie Graham write, "academic debates on cine-matic propaganda are almost entirely retrospective, and whilst a number of commentators have drawn attention to Hollywood's longstanding and open relationship with the Pentagon, little of substance has been written about the more clandestine influences working through Hollywood in the post-9/11 world."[1] Indeed, one of the greatest misconceptions about the CIA is that it purposely avoids all types of media exposure; in fact, as

Richard Aldrich points out, much of what we know about Langley has been deliberately placed in the public domain by the Agency itself, since it realizes the importance of controlling its public image.[2] By revealing what has, to date, remained a largely hidden history of the CIA in Hollywood, this project encourages readers to become more critical consumers of contemporary media and to further the academic conversation surrounding the modern government-entertainment complex.

But this book is not without its limitations. The CIA is far from an open organization, and many who work for the Agency remained tight-lipped about even the most basic information. Likewise, because the CIA has often preferred to communicate with theatrical agents through phone conversations rather than through e-mail or letters, and because many of its documents are exempt from Freedom of Information Act requests, the CIA rarely leaves a paper trail. Additionally, when Chase Brandon retired from his position as the CIA's entertainment liaison in 2006, he reportedly took with him every telephone number and piece of paper related to his job, and thus, as his successor Paul Barry explains, "nothing remains from the past (1995–late 2006)," leaving researchers with even less documentation to request and review.[3] As a result, the history of the CIA in Hollywood is, at present, more of a verbal history than a written one, which is complicated by the fact that those in Hollywood are often too busy, or simply unwilling, to speak with academic researchers about their collaborations with the government. Also, because the CIA's relationship with Hollywood involves "deep politics"—so called because they involve "activities which cannot currently be fully understood due to the covert influence of shadowy power players"[4]—this book cannot possibly claim to unveil all of the CIA's involvement in motion pictures over the past fifteen to twenty years; indeed, some of these collaborations may never be brought to light, while the exact nature of others will remain hidden. Instead, this book can only unveil a significant part of the CIA's hidden history in film and television, evaluate the impact of that history, and establish a strong foundation on which future investigations of the CIA in Hollywood may be based.

The Role and Structure of the CIA

Before delving into any analysis of the CIA's current involvement in Hollywood, it is important to briefly outline the structure and purpose of the Agency, and the extent to which it worked with the motion picture industry prior to the 1990s. The National Security Act of 1947 officially established the Central Intelligence Agency. The act, signed by President Truman, created a centralized intelligence organization aimed at correlating, evaluating, and disseminating information affecting national security. The information collected by the CIA assists military, executive, and legislative leaders in their decision-making processes. Unlike the FBI, which primarily collects information on American subjects, the CIA is sanctioned only to work abroad (although it can collect information on foreign subjects on U.S. soil). The CIA also has no "police, subpoena, law enforcement, or internal security functions."[5]

While the CIA's stated mission is to provide the president and congressional leaders with intelligence essential to national security, the Agency also engages in covert operations. Historically, these operations have included paramilitary activities and propaganda campaigns aimed at destabilizing and influencing opposing regimes, even during peacetime. The CIA uses secret funds to conduct these black operations under the premise of "plausible deniability," and while these activities are often controversial, it is important to remember that the CIA's covert capability is exercised at the direction of the president. No covert action is supposed to be undertaken without explicit presidential instruction or, as of the 1960s, a "finding," which is a legal authorization about which congressional overseers are made aware.

In order to accomplish its covert missions and its intelligence collection, the CIA has been divided into four sectors for most of its history. The National Clandestine Service (formerly called the Directorate of Operations) works to recruit and manage agents who provide the Agency with information, and it also attempts to influence or overthrow foreign governments, political parties, or leaders "through secret funding, training, paramilitary operations and propaganda."[6] The Directorate of Intelligence houses the Agency's analysts, who bring together information from human assets, satellites, television and radio broadcasts, newsletters, scientific publications, and more in order to make predictions about events and to inform policy makers. The third sector, the Directorate of Science and Technology, monitors satellite imagery, military communications, missile transmissions, and intercepted communications both within countries and inside foreign embassies. The directorate is also responsible for the creation of disguises and document forgeries, including foreign passports and birth certificates, for use by its assets and officers in the field. The final sector of the CIA is the Directorate of Support (formerly called the Directorate of Administration). Historically, this has been the CIA's largest department. In 1992, it housed roughly nine thousand employees, as opposed to the Directorate of Operations' five thousand, the Directorate of Intelligence's three thousand, and the Directorate of Science and Technology's five thousand employees.[7] These administrators, along with the Office of Human Resources, manage the Agency's payroll, office supply center, and money-laundering efforts. They also provide medical services for officers stationed overseas, manage the Agency's travel and transportation needs, assign security clearances, and work with the Agency's industrial partners in the corporate sector.[8] The directorate is also responsible for creating the Agency's global communications system and its information technology and security infrastructure.

Each of these directorates used to be managed by the director of central intelligence (DCI). The DCI served as the head of the CIA, coordinated other intelligence agencies in the government, and acted as the primary adviser to the president on foreign intelligence matters. In December 2004, however, President George W. Bush signed the Intelligence Reform and Terrorism Prevention Act, which restructured the intelligence community after the 9-11 Commission criticized its organization. This act abolished the position of the DCI as the coordinator of other intelligence agencies and gave those responsibilities to the newly created Office of the Director of National Intelligence. The act also changed the name of the DCI to the director of the Central Intelligence Agency (D/CIA), and this individual's only job is to now oversee the Agency and provide advice to policy makers.

One of the many tasks of the D/CIA is to hire and work with a director of public affairs (DPA) in order to communicate with the public (see table I.1). This director oversees the CIA's Public Affairs Office (PAO), which is responsible for handling Langley's internal communications and media requests from news organizations, academics, and entertainment professionals.[9] For the purposes of this book, it is important to emphasize that the majority of all Hollywood collaborators work in or through the PAO, and that from 1996 to 2008, the DPA oversaw the agency's entertainment industry liaison officers—Chase Brandon and Paul Barry—who were fully dedicated to assisting and influencing filmmakers and novelists. Upon Barry's departure in 2008, however, the PAO restructured its office, and now the responsibility of assisting moviemakers, writers, and television producers is divided among its four-person media relations team,

Table I.1. Recent Directors of the CIA and the Public Affairs Office

Directors of Central Intelligence (DCI) and Directors of the CIA (D/CIA)	Corresponding Director of Public Affairs	Corresponding Entertainment Industry Liaison Officer
Robert Gates 1991–1993	Gary Foster	None/responsibilities shared among the media relations team
James Woolsey 1993–1995	Kent Harrington	None/responsibilities shared among the media relations team
John Deutch 1995–1996	Dennis Boxx	Chase Brandon (hired in 1996)
George Tenet 1997–2004	Bill Harlow	Chase Brandon
Porter Goss 2004–2006	Jennifer Millerwise	Chase Brandon
Michael Hayden 2006–2009	Mark Mansfield	Brandon (left in 2007)/Paul Barry (2007–8)
Leon Panetta 2009–2011	Paul Gimigliano/ George Little	Position remains open/responsibilities shared among the media relations staff
David Petraeus	TBD	Position remains open/responsibilities shared among the media relations staff

although the position of entertainment liaison remained open as of the writing of this book.

The CIA in Hollywood during the Cold War

Because the CIA did not hire its first entertainment liaison until 1996, many have assumed that it was completely inactive in the film industry during the Cold War. This assumption is incorrect, as other Agency employees did work with filmmakers to carry out covert operations and propaganda campaigns. For example, Hugh Wilford explains in *The Mighty Wurlitzer* that the CIA was very interested in Hollywood during the Cold War because it believed films were the best medium through which to communicate pro-democratic messages in countries where illiteracy rates were high. Thus the CIA set out to influence several film productions by working with "intensely patriotic" and anticommunist players in the industry, including the filmmaker John Ford, the actor John Wayne, and the studio heads Cecil B. DeMille, Darryl Zanuck, and Luigi Luraschi.[10]

Indeed, the CIA's 1950s recruitment of Luraschi, the head of domestic and foreign censorship at Paramount Studios, proved productive, though short-lived. According to David Eldridge, Luraschi's job was to eliminate images that would offend foreign markets in the preproduction and production stages. He specifically worked to delete scenes where Americans were depicted as "brash, drunk, sexually immoral, violent or 'trigger-happy,'" and to eliminate others where Americans traveling abroad were depicted as imperialistic or insensitive to other cultures.[11] Luraschi worked to ensure that left-leaning films, such as *High Noon* (1952) and *The Little World of Don Camillo* (1952), were passed over for industry accolades, and he reported to the CIA on the political sympathies of other movie professionals.[12] Luraschi also worked with several casting directors to plant "well dressed negroes" into films, including "a dignified negro butler" who has lines "indicating he is a free man" in *Sangaree* (1953) and another in a golf scene in the 1953 film *The Caddy*.[13] These changes were not part of a campaign to instill what we now call "political correctness" in the populace, but were, as Alford and Graham write, "specifically enacted to hamper the Soviets' ability to exploit its enemy's poor record in race relations."[14]

The Office of Policy Coordination, a think tank housed at the CIA, also worked to discredit Soviet ideologies and counter communists' attacks on the West through film.[15] In the early 1950s, two members of the OPC's psychological warfare team who had dabbled in radio and film began negotiating with George Orwell's widow for the film rights to *Animal Farm*, his allegorical novella that painted an unflattering image of Stalin and the communist policies before World War II. According to Tony Shaw's *Hollywood's Cold War*, the novel was selected by the OPC because it could be turned into an animated film, which would be easily consumed by the illiterate in developing countries yet also be understood by industrial workers in more developed nations, where motion pictures played a larger cultural role.[16] That Orwell was a democratic socialist also distanced the film from right-leaning capitalists and could help disguise American backing of the project.

Orwell's widow, Sonia Blair, eventually agreed to sell the rights to Louis de Rochement's production company, RD-DR, with Carleton Alsop of the OPC likely acting as a go-between to finance and broker the deal.[17] De Rochement eventually contracted with a British animation company to produce the film since it would reduce costs, but also because "the lighter the American hand in the film, the greater its propaganda potential became."[18] While the film was never hugely successful, it did generate significant media attention and manipulated the ending of Orwell's book to drive home its anti-Soviet message,[19] thereby helping the CIA circulate pro-capitalist ideologies through film without the public ever knowing of its involvement. In fact, Daniel Leab, author of *Orwell Subverted*, points out that it took decades for the rumors about CIA involvement in *Animal Farm* to be properly documented, which "speaks volumes" about the Agency's abilities to keep its activities covert.[20]

By the late 1950s, the CIA had "grown adept at secretly financing the distribution of foreign-made films in regions of the world considered vulnerable to communism."[21] In fact, it repeated the feat by working alongside the Family Rosary Crusade's Father Patrick Peyton and the shipping magnate J. Peter Grace in 1958. Grace had asked the CIA to finance the dissemination of Peyton's Spanish-language "rosary films," which encouraged Catholicism, family unity, and prayer, since he believed "the strongest bulwark against communism was religion."[22] DCI Allen Dulles and Vice President Richard Nixon agreed to the proposal and provided the Family Rosary Crusade with $20,000 to launch a pilot program that showcased Peyton's films throughout Latin America.[23]

There were still further efforts to win hearts and minds. Through its Psychological Strategy Board, the CIA tried—without luck—to commission Frank Capra to direct a film series titled *Why We Fight the Cold War* and provided details to filmmakers about conditions in the USSR, in the hopes that they would use them in their movies.[24] More successfully, the CIA-supervised American Committee for Cultural Freedom oversaw the production of the Michael Redgrave feature *1984* (1956),[25] and the Agency was able to influence the 1958 film version of *The Quiet American*. Edward Lansdale, a legendary CIA operative, specifically helped the writer and director of the latter film, Joseph Mankiewicz, to "reverse the anti-Americanism" of Graham Greene's novel and turn it "into a decidedly patriotic film."[26] The pair's revisions included an alternate ending, where the communists, rather than the American-backed Colonel Thé, are responsible for a terrorist bombing in Saigon. The two also reveal that the communists have tricked Thomas Fowler into murdering the quiet American, Alden Pyle, who turns out not to be a weapons runner (as he is in the novel and as film viewers had been led to believe), but rather a manufacturer of children's toys. Upon the film's completion, Lansdale wrote to President Ngo Dinh Diem that the film was an excellent change from "Greene's novel of despair" and should help the American-backed president "win more friends . . . [in] Vietnam [and] in many places in the world where it is shown."[27]

As Harry Rositzke explains in *The CIA's Secret Operations*, the heyday for CIA covert propaganda campaigns ran throughout the 1950s and into the early 1960s but eventually declined by the end of the decade.[28] Nonetheless, the CIA did continue to use film and filmmakers during the later stages of the Cold War. Tony Mendez, a retired CIA officer, recalls that any time a Soviet official visited the United States, the Agency made sure he or she left with VHS players, computers, fashion magazines, and films in order to spur the Soviets' desire for capitalism. Mendez also claimed that the CIA's covert action programs often "had a very robust media component," and that its "Mighty Wurlitzer"[29] program "co-opted a lot of showbiz people who were used as ambassadors of the West."[30] The CIA officer Paul Barry likewise explained that the Agency "pumped" dozens of episodes of *Dynasty* (1981–1989) into East Germany during the Cold War in order to sell those residents on capitalism and the luxury life it could afford.[31]

The CIA also worked with filmmakers to carry out its covert operations. Mendez, a former disguise master, has often recounted how the famous makeup artist John Chambers[32] worked as a consultant with the Headquarters Disguise Unit to develop new techniques.[33] Chambers, at the time of his collaboration, was at the apex of his career, having just won an Academy Award for his makeup artistry on *Planet of the Apes* (1968). For that film, Chambers had developed a malleable material that could be applied to actors' arms and faces to make their disguises look more realistic, even from reasonably close distances. His developments, which he shared with the CIA, were then further developed for use in the field. In one case, the Agency even used the material to transform an Asian statesman and an African American case officer into two Caucasians, which helped the men continue their clandestine meetings without attracting much attention in Vientiane, Laos.[34]

But Hollywood's makeup artists did not stop at helping the CIA to develop disguise materials. The collaboration with Chambers again proved extremely useful in 1979, when a group of Islamic militants took over the U.S. embassy in Tehran in support of the Iranian Revolution. Between November 1979 and January 1981, roughly fifty Americans were held hostage, but six were able to escape the embassy and enter into hiding before the takeover was complete. In *Master of Disguise*, Mendez recounts how the CIA was able to extract these six men and women from the country by disguising them as a Hollywood film crew. "In the intelligence business," he writes, "we usually try to match cover legends closely to the actual experience of the person involved. A cover should be bland, as uninteresting as possible, so the casual observer, or the not-so-casual immigration official, doesn't probe too deeply."[35] The situation in Tehran, however, was unusual, and Mendez believed that disguising the men and women as a film crew might work precisely because no sensible spy organization would be suspected of using it.[36]

In order to build a convincing cover for the Americans, Mendez and his team worked with Chambers and fellow makeup artist Bob Sidell to establish a fake Hollywood production company called Studio Six Productions, which soon announced its first project—a movie titled *Argo* to be shot in Iran. The front company soon took out trade advertisements announcing the film's production in both *Variety* and the *Hollywood Reporter* to strengthen the cover of the six Americans, who would eventually pose as members of a production crew surveying the country for shooting locations, transportation logistics, and more. The fake production company was so convincing that it had acquired twenty-eight scripts from screenwriters during the time it was open, including submissions from Steven Spielberg and George Lucas.[37]

Mendez, Chambers, and Sidell kept Studio Six running until March of 1980, six weeks after the small American group arrived home safely, because the CIA believed that it might be able to use the *Argo* project to send larger production crews into Iran in the future. The production crews, of course, would really be composed of Delta Force members who would then rescue the remaining hostages through military action, but the Agency never carried out this plan.[38] The Hollywood community never learned about the CIA's deception until seventeen years later when the Agency asked Mendez to tell his story. George Clooney's Smoke House production company is now scheduled to turn the story of the operation into a dramedy with Warner Bros. backing. The film, originally called *Escape from Tehran* but now titled *Argo*, is a joint effort between Clooney and Grant Heslov and Ben Affleck is currently slated as both the director and star.

These examples do not cover all of the CIA's work during the Cold War, but they are representative, since each demonstrates that the Agency collaborated with the entertainment industry to promote American ideologies abroad and formulated an alliance with trusted artists to help carry out covert operations. The end of the Cold War, however, brought about a rapid and dramatic shift in the CIA's relationship with Hollywood. Instead of using motion pictures for psychological warfare directed at communists living abroad, the Agency primarily began to use film and television to improve *its own* public image at home. This shift in focus was complete by the mid-1990s, when Langley hired its first entertainment industry liaison officer and had an officially backed television series in development. In order to understand why this shift took place and how the CIA now works to affect popular media, the rest of this book explores the CIA's post–Cold War and post-9/11 involvement in the entertainment industry.

Outline of This Book's Structure

Because the CIA often claims that it began working with Hollywood to reverse its negative image in film and television, *The CIA in Hollywood* begins by providing an overview of how the American motion picture industry has historically depicted the Agency. The first chapter, "Rogues, Assassins, and Buffoons," specifically explains that the CIA has been represented in five main ways: As an outfit (1) intent on assassination, (2) comprising rogue operatives who act with little oversight, (3) failing to take care of its own officers and assets, (4) operating on morally ambiguous and perhaps morally reprehensible grounds, or (5) bedeviled by its own buffoonery and hopeless disorganization. The chapter then explains how the CIA's actual history, the demands of cinematic storytelling, and the political nature of the Hollywood community have all contributed to these representations, before arguing that such negative images are only part of the reason for the CIA's current involvement in Hollywood—even though they are, by far, the most cited.

Chapter 2, "Opening the Doors," picks up on this thread by explaining why the CIA's negative image in film and television grew to be of greater concern during the end of the Cold War and the Aldrich Ames case of 1994. These two events were what primarily caused the CIA to establish a formal relationship with filmmakers in the mid-1990s and led to its first major Hollywood collaboration—a little-known television series called *The Classified Files of the CIA* that was heavily modeled after ABC and J. Edgar Hoover's television series *The FBI*. The chapter then explains why the CIA hired Chase Brandon as its first entertainment liaison in 1996, outlines what this job entailed, and unveils how the CIA is now able to influence texts in both the production and preproduction stages of filmmaking.

The third chapter, "Necessary and Competent," takes an in-depth look at two of the CIA's earliest collaborations that actually made it to viewers: Showtime's film *In the Company of Spies* and the CBS television series *The Agency*. Both of these projects were granted unprecedented access to CIA personnel and Agency headquarters for filming, and were even scheduled to premiere at red-carpet events at Langley. Drawing on internal CIA documents and interviews with the shows' writers, technical consultants, and assistant producers, this chapter outlines the exact nature of support that the CIA lent these projects. Further, I explore how that support helped improve Langley's image at a time when the news media were either highly critical of the CIA's intelligence gathering or questioning the need for the Agency's very existence. The chapter also explains how Chase Brandon worked with *The Agency*'s creator to intimidate terrorists through the show's narratives and may have even used the series to workshop threat scenarios on the CIA's behalf.

Building on the information presented in the previous chapter, chapter 4, "The Chase Brandon Years," explores several other post-9/11 media collaborations in order to demonstrate further the scope and nature of the CIA's relationship with Hollywood. Placing a special emphasis on *Enemy of the State*, *The Sum of All Fears*, *Alias*, and *The Recruit*, this chapter specifically explains the CIA's motivations for working in Hollywood, especially as they relate to recruitment, intimidating or misinforming its enemies, improving its public image, and boosting employee morale and its industry connections.

Perhaps the most critical chapter of this book, chapter 5, "The Legal and Ethical Implications of the CIA in Hollywood," engages with many of the legal and ethical issues at play within CIA-Hollywood collaborations. More specifically, it argues that the CIA's refusal to support all filmmakers seeking its assistance constitutes a violation of the First Amendment's right to free speech. The chapter also posits that CIA efforts in Hollywood should be defined as propaganda, rather than the educational campaigns that the CIA often claims them to be, and that Langley's actions violate the spirit, if not the letter, of the publicity and propaganda laws, which forbid the government from engaging in self-aggrandizing and covert communication.

Chapter 6, "The Last People We Want in Hollywood," takes a departure from officially assisted works to analyze the role of retired CIA officers in Hollywood, exploring the advantages and drawbacks of their work from the perspectives of the viewers, filmmakers, and the CIA itself. The chapter focuses heavily on Milt Bearden and Robert Baer's work on *The*

Good Shepherd, *Syriana*, and, to a lesser extent, *Charlie Wilson's War* as case studies. Because Agency retirees have no obligation to provide a positive or even fair image of Langley, the CIA has often claimed that retirees are the "last people" they want to represent them in Hollywood. The CIA's dissatisfaction with retirees has also been compounded by the fact that some of their most successful collaborations have fallen into the category of the docudrama, causing viewers to see these more negative films as historically accurate. As such, this chapter explores the CIA flak aimed at discrediting these men and their films, but it ultimately argues that their work in Hollywood is actually valuable. A brief conclusion that highlights many of the book's main ideas follows.

In total, then, this book aims to give readers a look at the CIA-Hollywood relationship from multiple perspectives and to explore an under-studied topic. It is my hope that *The CIA in Hollywood* will also encourage more critical media consumption and shed additional light on the topic of government propaganda.

Rogues, Assassins, and Buffoons: Representations of the CIA in Film and Television

The CIA often claims that it opened its doors to Hollywood in the 1990s because it had had enough of the way filmmakers depicted the Agency. In 2001, for example, the *New York Times* reported that Langley finally decided to reverse its policy of rejecting requests from producers for consultation because it was "tired of being depicted on screen as a nefarious organization full of rogue operatives."[1] Chase Brandon, the Agency's first entertainment liaison, added that "year after year, as moviegoers and TV watchers, we've seen our image and our reputation constantly sullied with egregious, ugly misrepresentations of who we are and what we stand for. We've been imbued with these extraordinary Machiavellian conspiratorial capabilities."[2] He also claimed that when he had a chance to make the Agency "more accessible to people who created our image," he took it because he could no longer stand seeing his colleagues depicted "as backstabbing assassins full of deceit and treachery."[3] In a 2007 story about Paul Barry, Brandon's successor, the *Washington Post* likewise reported that Barry was continuing to try to reverse "those crazed-rogue-agents portrayals of the Agency" and to promote a different and broader picture of the outfit.[4]

In each of these examples, the CIA and the media imply that the Agency has long been the victim of an ill-intentioned and misinformed Hollywood community. But exactly how has Hollywood depicted the CIA in film and television in both the Cold War and post-9/11 eras? And where do some of the CIA's most negative portrayals come from anyway? The general answer is that the CIA did not appear in popular film and television until the 1960s, and since that time, its representations have fallen into five main categories, each reflecting a public concern about Langley. As mentioned in the introduction, these include the worries that (1) the

CIA assassinates people (often without good reason), (2) it is staffed by rogue operatives who act with little oversight, (3) it fails to take care of its own officers and assets, (4) the outfit operates on morally ambiguous and perhaps morally reprehensible grounds, and (5) that it is marked by buffoonery and ineffectiveness.

These representations are partially the result of both the demands of cinematic storytelling and the political nature of the Hollywood community. But they also stem from the actual history of the CIA and its culture of secrecy. Thus, while the Agency is justified in pointing out its unbalanced representation in film and television, it is not justified in setting itself up as a victim of Hollywood. In order to understand how these conclusions can be reached, a more detailed discussion of each argument follows.

The Historical Roots of the CIA's Image in Film and Television

Spy films have existed since at least the 1920s; an early example is Fritz Lang's *Spione* (1928), which featured disappearing ink and agents known only by numbers. Alfred Hitchcock furthered the popularity of the genre in the 1930s with thrillers like *The Man Who Knew Too Much* (1934), *The 39 Steps* (1935), and *The Lady Vanishes* (1938), while the 1940s and 1950s featured several films about the exploits of Allied agents in occupied Europe. Not until the early 1960s, however, was the Central Intelligence Agency featured in mainstream film or television. The barrage of negative images soon followed.

Providing an astute summary in 2006, Erik Lundegaard argues that since its inception in 1947, the CIA has rarely been "front and center" in Hollywood films, and when it does appear on-screen, its representatives generally "skulk along the edges and in the shadows."[5] Yet even in this capacity, the CIA is primarily depicted as keeping tabs on famous citizens (*Malcolm X*), using innocent people as pawns (*Ishtar*), hanging its own agents out to dry (*Spy Game*), assassinating foreign and military leaders (*Syriana* and *Apocalypse Now*) and possibly the president of the United States (*JFK*) (see Table 1.1). "They can be blazingly efficient" or "buffoonishly incompetent," Lundegaard writes, but either way, "they are always dangerous."[6]

Bill Harlow, a former director of public affairs at the CIA, echoed Lundegaard when he argued that the entertainment industry has traditionally typecast Agency officers as "evil, terrible, malicious folks," citing *In the Line of Fire* as a perfect example.[7] Chase Brandon has likewise

Table 1.1. A Sample of Films and Television Series Featuring the CIA and Its Officers

---

1960s	*Dr. No* (1962), *Goldfinger* (1964), *The Ipcress File* (1965), *Operation C.I.A.* (1965), *Thunderball* (1965)
1970s	*The Kremlin Letter* (1970), *Diamonds Are Forever* (1971), *H-Bomb* (1971), *Madame Sin* (1972), *Executive Action* (1973), *Key West* (1973), *Live and Let Die* (1973), *Scorpio* (1973), *The Spook Who Sat by the Door* (1973), *Three Days of the Condor* (1975), *M*A*S*H* (1972–83), *Avalanche Express* (1979)
1980s	*Hopscotch* (1980), *The Amateur* (1981), *Condorman* (1981), *The Soldier* (1982), *Wrong Is Right* (1982), *The Osterman Weekend* (1983), *Ninja in the Claw of the CIA* (1983), *The Man with One Red Shoe* (1985), *Spies Like Us* (1985), *Jumpin' Jack Flash* (1986), *Ishtar* (1987), *Malone* (1987), *Mankillers* (1987), *License to Kill* (1989)
1990s	*The Hunt for Red October* (1990), *JFK* (1991), *CIA Codename: Alexa* (1992), *Malcolm X* (1992), *Patriot Games* (1992), *CIA: Exiled* (1993), *In the Line of Fire* (1993), *CIA II: Target Alexa* (1994), *Clear and Present Danger* (1994), *Femme Fontaine: Killer Babe for the C.I.A.* (1994), *GoldenEye* (1995), *To the Limit* (1995), *Mission: Impossible* (1996), *Black Sea Raid* (1997), *Dead Men Can't Dance* (1997), *Tomorrow Never Dies* (1997), *Ronin* (1998), *The Siege* (1999)
2000s	*Company Man* (2000), *Falcon Down* (2000), *Meet the Parents* (2000), *Mission: Impossible II* (2000), *The Agency* (2001–3), *Alias* (2001–6), *Spy Game* (2001), *Spy Kids* (2001), *24* (2001–10), *Bad Company* (2002), *The Bourne Identity* (2002), *Collateral Damage* (2002), *Confessions of a Dangerous Mind* (2002), *Die Another Day* (2002), *The Quiet American* (2002), *The Sum of All Fears* (2002), *Agent Cody Banks* (2003), *1st Testament: CIA Vengeance* (2003), *Once upon a Time in Mexico* (2003), *The Recruit* (2003), *Agent Cody Banks 2* (2004), *The Bourne Supremacy* (2004), *Meet the Fockers* (2004), *American Dad!* (2005–), *Syriana* (2005), *Casino Royale* (2006), *The Good Shepherd* (2006), *Mission: Impossible III* (2006), *Burn Notice* (2007–), *The Bourne Ultimatum* (2007), *Charlie Wilson's War* (2007), *Chuck* (2007–), *The Company* (2007), *Body of Lies* (2008), *Burn after Reading* (2008), *Nothing but the Truth* (2008), *Quantum of Solace* (2008), *The Objective* (2009), *Taken* (2009), *Covert Affairs* (2010–), *The Ghost Writer* (2010), *Green Zone* (2010), *Salt* (2010), *Undercovers* (2010)

---

pointed out that villains in political thrillers tend to be ex-CIA operatives or rogue operatives: "They are always fomenting revolution or serving as hit men. There is always some ugly representation of us as a conspiratorial government overthrow apparatus."[8] The United International Press reviewer Steve Sailer also argues that while the FBI's early relationship with Hollywood led to films "full of heroic G-men," the CIA's early refusal to work with the motion picture industry led to films where "CIA higher-ups were almost always portrayed as cruel, devious, and incompetent uber-WASPs with thin lips and thinning hair."[9] Of course, the CIA has been depicted negatively in films for reasons other than its early refusal to work with Hollywood, but these writers and spokespeople are right in pointing out that the historical image of the CIA has primarily been a negative one—and, as outlined above, these negative images fit into five basic categories.

Category One: The CIA Assassinates People

CIA historians deny that there is any historical basis for its negative image in film and TV,[10] but this is simply not the case. For example, one of the most frequent images of the CIA revolves around the public concern that the Agency assassinates people, even though its PAO often states that the CIA does not engage in "wet" work,[11] and Executive Order 12333 clearly states that "no person employed by or acting on behalf of the United States Government shall engage in, or conspire to engage in, assassination."[12] In reality, though, the CIA does engage in what it now calls "lethal findings." In 2002, for instance, President George W. Bush signed a secret finding authorizing the CIA to kill suspected terrorists overseas, including those with U.S. citizenship.[13] That finding authorized the Agency to use a Predator drone missile strike to kill six suspected al-Qaeda leaders in Yemen, including Qaed Salim Sinan al-Harethi and an American citizen, Kamal Derwish. Under the Obama administration, the CIA has launched a number of drone attacks in Pakistan, targeting and killing suspected Taliban leaders.

The Agency's history of attempted assassination, however, dates back to the 1950s, when it launched a campaign against the president of Guatemala, Jacobo Arbenz, for his programs of economic reform. Declassified memos reveal that as early as February 1952, Langley began generating reports that outlined categories of people to be neutralized through executive action in Guatemala, with the "A" list of those to be "assassinated containing 58 names" in total.[14] The 1970s Church Committee reports further revealed the CIA's assassination attempts of Patrice Lumumba in the Congo, Fidel Castro in Cuba, the Diem brothers of Vietnam, and Gen. René Schneider of Chile throughout the 1960s.[15]

As a result of this history, Hollywood has employed many plots involving CIA assassins, which appear in films such as *Scorpio* (1973), *Three Days of the Condor* (1975), *The Amateur* (1981), *The Osterman Weekend* (1983),

JFK (1991), *In the Line of Fire* (1993), the Jason Bourne trilogy (2000s), *Confessions of a Dangerous Mind* (2002), *Syriana* (2005), and *The Good Shepherd* (2006), to name just a few. Even B-grade features such as *Femme Fontaine: Killer Babe for the C.I.A.* (1994) have used the stereotype. The primary concern reflected by this entertainment stereotype is not so much that the CIA assassinates people, however; it is more the fear that Langley assassinates innocent people, kills others just for holding an opposing ideology or getting in the CIA's way, and that these killings damage the moral sanctity of the United States.

Syriana, for instance, features the Agency killing an Arab prince because it suspects that he is a terrorist, when in reality he is a Western-educated intellectual set on implementing capitalist and democratic reforms. The film, therefore, depicts the CIA taking out one of its best hopes for change in the Middle East, not to mention ending an innocent man's life, simply because it acted on bad information. Oliver Stone's *JFK* also reflects fears about the CIA's assassinations when it suggests that the Agency played a role in the murder of President Kennedy because it felt that his administration had become too left-leaning. *Scorpio* likewise shows the Agency assassinating its own operative simply because he knows too much about its covert operations, a theme that is repeated in *The Bourne Identity*, when Langley attempts to kill the former dictator Nykwana Wombosi because he has threatened to publicly reveal information about the CIA's illegal activities in Africa unless he is returned to power.

In fact, throughout the Jason Bourne trilogy, the CIA engages in numerous assassinations and suggests that Bourne is just one of several operatives the CIA has in place throughout the world for this purpose. In the first installment of the series, Bourne develops amnesia to protect his psyche from the guilt he incurs from engaging in frequent wet work, and when the spy finally remembers how he was programmed as an assassin by the Agency, he works to free himself of its control—efforts that end in the death of CIA administrators, the public exposure of its assassination program, and an impending criminal investigation against its leaders. The theme of the CIA's efforts coming back to haunt it is also present in Wolfgang Petersen's *In the Line of Fire*. This film features John Malkovich as Mitch Leary, a CIA assassin intent on killing the president of the United States after suffering a mental breakdown partly caused by his longtime Agency service.

Both *In the Line of Fire* and the Bourne trilogy imply that assassinations are anathema to the mental health of those who carry them out, and thus organizations that encourage their usage should be prepared for their trainees to turn against them. More broadly, all these films suggest that assassinations prevent the United States from taking the moral high road in international debates, as they expose both the corrupt and self-interested motives that often lie behind such killings and the nation's failure to peacefully coexist with those holding opposing viewpoints. These films also suggest that assassinations often lead to further domestic and global instability (as evidenced by *In the Line of Fire* and *JFK*) and that the CIA would probably do best to abandon the practice.

Category Two: The CIA Is Composed of Rogue Operatives

In the same vein, several films have depicted the CIA as plagued by rogue operatives, who, because they act with little oversight, often jeopardize their colleagues and country. In fact, many of the films that feature CIA assassins also fall into the "rogue" category, including *Three Days of the Condor*, which features Robert Redford as the CIA analyst Joe Turner. This 1975 film opens with Turner returning from lunch to find everyone in his office dead, and when he calls his superior to ask for protection, the men who arrive to "help" him also try to kill him. As the plot nears its climax, it becomes clear that a rogue element inside the CIA is trying to murder Turner, believing that he has discovered its secret plan to seize control of the Middle East's oil fields. Rather than trust Turner with the secret (which he doesn't even know he's discovered), the rogue CIA element simply decides it's best to eliminate its own colleague.

The rogue theme was repeated in 1981's *The Amateur*, in which John Savage plays the CIA analyst Charles Heller, whose fiancée is killed in a terrorist attack in Munich. After the CIA refuses to kill the terrorists and avenge her death, Heller blackmails the Agency, forcing it to train him as an assassin so he can commit the murders himself. Of course, what Heller uses as blackmail are memos and reports documenting the CIA's illegal activities, including a possible attempt by the CIA to assassinate the prime minister of Kuwait. The CIA, which has lied to the Senate oversight committee about its operations, appeases Heller in order to keep its operations unknown.

Other films have also featured rogue elements within the CIA, including *Clear and Present Danger* (1994), *To the Limit* (1995), *Mission: Impossible* (1996), *The Recruit* (2003), and *Salt* (2010). For instance, while *Clear and Present Danger* depicted Jack Ryan and the ailing DCI in a positive light, it still used Robert Ritter, the CIA's deputy director of operations, and James Cutter, the national security adviser, as the film's primary nemeses. At the start of this film, the two work to take out a major Colombian drug cartel by sending in a covert action unit behind Ryan's back, even though Ryan is now in charge of the Agency. Later, the two agree to give up the location of that same paramilitary unit when an aspiring drug lord agrees to assassinate the current cartel leader, take his place, and then reduce the cocaine traffic into the United States by 50 percent, so that the president can take credit for winning the war on drugs. When Ryan learns about the plot, he goes to Colombia to help John Clark, the team coordinator, locate and rescue the soldiers, but Ritter and Cutter tell Clark that Ryan was responsible for the operations' shutdown, hoping that Clark will murder Ryan in anger. While this fails to happen, Ritter is still depicted as attempting to assassinate his own colleague in order to cover up his own wrongdoing, and as abandoning his country's own covert operatives in order to help the president achieve a purely political goal—all in a rogue capacity.

The roots of the rogue operative in film and television are not as easy to trace as the CIA-as-assassin representation, but they are likely grounded in the public's mistaken understanding that the Agency operates with little to no civilian oversight. In reality, the CIA is overseen by the executive branch, through the National Security Council, while the Senate Select Committee on Intelligence and the House Permanent Select Committee on Intelligence also monitor the Agency regularly. Nonetheless, stories intermittently appear that indicate the Agency is able to work on initiatives that evade congressional oversight. Such was the case in 2009, when Senate Intelligence Committee Chairwoman Dianne Feinstein censured the CIA for breaking the law by failing to notify Congress about its secret assassination program. This program, launched in 2004, conspired to use the security firm Blackwater/Xe to locate and assassinate top operatives of al-Qaeda.[16]

Additionally, David Barrett points out in *The CIA and Congress* that congressional oversight of the CIA from 1947 until 1961 was much more informal, and Barrett found no records that indicated the CIA briefed Congress in advance of any specific covert action until the Bay of Pigs. Concerns about the CIA's lack of oversight also appeared in 1974 when Seymour Hersh reported on the Agency's illegal surveillance of American citizens.[17] His revelations, along with William Colby's memo to Henry Kissinger documenting the Agency's broader efforts to subvert foreign governments and assassinate foreign leaders, led to the Church Committee congressional investigation in the mid-1970s and the pronouncement that CIA oversight had been too relaxed.[18]

Such histories have certainly helped to generate and perpetuate the image in films of the CIA as a rogue entity. For instance, James Grady, author of *Six Days of the Condor*, on which *Three Days of the Condor* is based, argues that the image of the CIA as a rogue group "began to emerge after their 'roguishness' was revealed by Watergate and the Church Committee and Pentagon Papers. (And yeah, the movie *Three Days of the Condor*.) Add that to what seems to be an endemic American paranoia . . . [and] what you get is the anti-government fears of America pasted on an Agency's face that both thrills and scares us with its supposed ability to reach out and . . . kill. Throw in copy-cat writing that is a hallmark of Hollywood and lazy popular fiction, and you've got the 'rogue' reputation."[19]

As Grady suggests, the CIA's history has played into both the creation and interpretation of CIA-related films—a point echoed by *Condor*'s director, Sidney Pollack. In a 1976 interview, Pollack explained that the film's release intersected so perfectly with the Church Committee reports that critics couldn't help but interpret the film as a political commentary on the CIA's rogue nature. When Pollack was asked to comment on the film's politicized ending, he also noted that while he allowed the CIA to explain its actions in the film, he still believed that "we have to find some way of making a check and balance system work that, conceivably, hasn't been working before. The CIA has grown autonomous in a way that's horrific."[20] Although *Condor* entered into production before the Church reports were even made public and thus the film could not have been intended as a warning about the autonomy of the Agency, Pollack's comments nonetheless worked to link, in the public's mind, the film's depiction of the CIA as a rogue entity to the CIA's actual history, and to point to the ways that history and film intersect to reinforce popular images of the Agency.

Category Three: The CIA Fails to Take Care of Its Own

Like *Three Days of the Condor*, which features the CIA trying to kill its own analyst, *Scorpio* depicts the Agency trying to eliminate its own officers after their usefulness has expired. The film stars Burt Lancaster as Cross, a CIA assassin trying to retire from the Agency in order to spend more time with his wife. As the film progresses, viewers learn that the CIA wants Cross's protégé, Scorpio, to assassinate his mentor because he knows too much about their covert operations. Scorpio, who has been tricked into killing Cross, eventually carries out his assignment, but not before Cross hints that he, too, will be killed when the CIA no longer finds him useful. And, indeed, as Scorpio leaves the scene of the crime, he is felled by a sniper's bullet.

Spy Game (2001) features a very different plotline but nonetheless suggests that the CIA fails to take care of its own. In this film, the United States is on the verge of sealing a major trade agreement with the Chinese government. Unfortunately, during the same period, Langley learns that one of its field officers, Tom Bishop (Brad Pitt), has been captured while trying to free the woman he loves from a Chinese prison. Bishop is set to be executed by the Chinese unless he is claimed by the U.S. government, which refuses to intervene since it would risk destroying the trade deal and because Bishop was operating in a rogue capacity when he broke into the prison. As a result, the CIA calls in Bishop's former mentor, Nathan Muir (Robert Redford), to provide them with more information on Bishop that might justify the CIA letting him die. Muir then acts in a rogue capacity to save Bishop minutes before his scheduled execution—one of the few times in such films that a rogue operation is actually championed by viewers.

Images of the CIA hanging its own assets out to dry have also appeared in post-9/11 films. To cite just one example, *Body of Lies* (2008) stars Leonardo DiCaprio as an Arabic-speaking field officer operating in the Middle East and Russell Crowe as a Langley-based bureaucrat. Neither character is admirable, but DiCaprio's actions are often the most egregious—especially as he kills a captured asset to protect his own identity, and sets up an innocent businessman, without his knowledge or consent, as a "decoy" terrorist in order to locate a real one. DiCaprio's character gives little thought about what the setup will mean for the businessman's life, or the fact that the hoax will eventually lead to the man's execution. In other words, DiCaprio's character fails to appreciate the human costs of spying, using and discarding assets without sympathy.

Part of this representation likely stems from the fact that if caught, the U.S. government has historically failed to acknowledge its officers' CIA status for fear of compromising a larger mission or overall diplomatic relations. The idea that the CIA will go so far as to hunt down its own officers and assets to protect its interests simply pushes the concept to an extreme in order to ask how far any outfit should go to carry out its agenda (and, admittedly, just for dramatic effect).

The CIA historian Nicholas Dujmovic is quick to point out, though, that the government's failure to acknowledge someone's CIA status and the Agency's failure to take care of its people are two different things. He specifically points to the case of two CIA officers who were captured by the Chinese in the 1950s and not released until the 1970s. During their captivity, the government failed to acknowledge the men's CIA status, but behind the scenes the Agency ensured that the officers continued to receive salaries and earn pay raises, and also assisted the officers' aging parents and their children's educational pursuits.[21] As a result, Dujmovic believes that "the mythology that CIA fails to take care of its own is used by Hollywood because it's simply perceived as a more interesting story that fits in with [stereotypes about] how callous and immoral we are."[22]

Category Four: The CIA as Morally Bankrupt

As Dujmovic's comments and many of the above plotlines suggest, Hollywood often encourages viewers to believe that the CIA attracts people with a diminished ability to discern between right and wrong, or that the lines of right and wrong cannot help but become blurred in the shadowy world of intelligence. Either way, with its assassins, infidelity, and illegal operations, the CIA has often been typecast as operating on morally ambiguous grounds.

Undoubtedly, the CIA's own history plays into this depiction. For instance, it has been revealed that the Agency tested LSD on unsuspecting American citizens in order to gauge the drug's application in psychological warfare through the program MKULTRA—a fact alluded to in *The Good Shepherd* when the CIA tests LSD on a suspected disinformation agent, and the "truth serum" causes him to die by defenestration. From the 1950s to 1973, the CIA (and FBI) also intercepted, opened, and photographed thousands of letters behind the postal service's back, and the idea that the CIA continues similar practices has reappeared in several texts, including an episode of *Alias* (2001–2006). In "A Higher Echelon," a CIA employee explains to viewers that the Agency currently monitors most Americans' faxes, e-mails, and phone calls—or, more to the point, violates their constitutional rights to privacy and the CIA's jurisdiction.

In the 1970s and 1980s, the CIA again muddied its reputation through its involvement in the Watergate and Iran-Contra scandals.[23] In more recent years, the outfit has come under fire for its use of waterboarding, torture, and private interrogation camps; its destruction of interrogation tapes; and its practice of extraordinary rendition. In fact, in November 2009, an Italian judge convicted twenty-three Americans—including the CIA's Milan station chief, Robert Seldon Lady—of kidnapping Hassan Osama Nasr, an Egyptian cleric. Nasr was taken off the streets of Milan in 2003 and flown to Egypt, where he claims to have undergone months of torture and abuse. The case sparked an international uproar, with the lead prosecutor praising the court's guilty verdict for sending the message that "we cannot use illegal instruments in our effort against terrorism. Our democracies, otherwise, would betray their principles."[24]

Unsurprisingly, these issues have each been the subject of recent films and television programs. For instance, *Rendition* (2007) stars Reese Witherspoon as the wife of Anwar El-Ibrahimi, an American resident the CIA suspects is linked to a terrorist bombing in North Africa. In order to find out more about Anwar, the Agency kidnaps, tortures, and holds him without trial or charge, even when the evidence suggests he is innocent. The film's screenwriter, Kelley Sane, admits that he used news stories about rendition to develop his story lines and claims that the piece is meant to serve as an entertaining commentary on post-9/11 policies. "One side of me understands how people in power want to use every instrument at their disposal to protect Americans and to show potential foes . . . that we're tough," he stated. "But the other side is the bigger picture, which is when we take our gloves off and lose our moral foundation, then we become less powerful. . . . So that was kind of the idea when I first started putting this idea together."[25]

While post-9/11 and 1970s spy texts are the most likely to feature the CIA as a morally bankrupt agency, it is important to note that this strain has run throughout the decades, making it one of the most consistent characterizations. Numerous 1980s films, for instance, focus on the fear that the CIA uses innocent people as unsuspecting pawns, including *The Osterman Weekend* (1983), *Ishtar* (1987), and *The Man with One Red Shoe* (1985). Indeed, this last film features Deputy Director Cooper launching a smear campaign against Director of Central Intelligence Ross in order to obtain his job. When Ross learns of the plan, he leaks false information that a man is arriving by plane to clear his name. Ross then instructs his lackey to pick an arriving passenger at random in order to lead his nemesis on a wild goose chase. Of course, the "comedy" ensues when the lackey selects the violinist Richard Drew (Tom Hanks) and Cooper comes to believe that he is carrying a coded message in his sheet music. When the deputy director's team fails to decode the music or uncover any useful information about Drew, Cooper attempts to murder the musician. Thus Drew becomes another unwitting pawn wrapped up in the dangerous power struggles of the CIA.

Category Five: The CIA as Buffoonish and Hopelessly Ineffective

As this last film suggests, the CIA is often depicted as lethal, even in comedies, but it is sometimes depicted as incompetent and even hopelessly buffoonish. For instance, on the hit series *M*A*S*H* (1972–1983), Colonel Flagg (Edward Winter) is an idiotic intelligence operative who often claims to work for the CIA. Flagg is best described as overly paranoid, once accusing Major Burns of being a communist because he reads *Reader's Digest*, which spells *Red's Digest* "if you take out the third, fifth, and sixth letters." His disguises are also so poor that his colleagues see through them immediately, and Flagg purposely injures himself on several occasions in order to achieve his agendas, making him appear mentally unstable at best.

The television series *Get Smart* (1965–1970) likewise parodied the CIA through Don Adams's portrayal of Maxwell Smart. Adams is essentially the anti-James Bond—an operative with a grinding, nasally voice, a propensity to be distracted, and a host of technological devices that either fail to work (e.g., the "Cone of Silence") or work at precisely the wrong moment (e.g., the shoe phone). While Smart served as a CONTROL agent rather than as a CIA operative, the series cocreator Mel Brooks often drew parallels between the two outfits, helping viewers read the series as a spoof of the CIA. In fact, Brooks once argued that one of *Get Smart*'s main messages is to "never trust a government agency that uses the word covert," adding that the "CIA always—because of the word *covert*—allowed themselves to do things without Congress or the administration," making them "very dangerous people."26

The representation of a buffoonish CIA continued in the 1980s with films like *Hopscotch* (1980) and *Spies Like Us* (1985), the latter of which suggested that even the below-average Joe is more adept at fighting the Cold War than the actual CIA. Such representations are also present in post-9/11 texts, as evidenced by *American Dad!* (2005–), a satirical animated series on Fox. Like *M*A*S*H*, this series features an overly paranoid CIA operative working for an inept organization. In "Francine's Flashback," for instance, Agent Stan Smith forgets his wedding anniversary, so he asks the CIA to erase twenty hours of his wife's memory; the Agency screws up and accidentally erases twenty years. Additionally, one of the series' characters, a goldfish named Klaus, is the result of a nefarious CIA experiment that features the Agency exchanging brains between the fish and a German man.

The historical roots of the CIA as incompetent may rest in the fact that while a few 1950s films featured members of the Office of Strategic Services (the CIA's precursor), it was not until the 1960s that the CIA began appearing in film and television regularly. As the CIA historian Gary McCollim explains, 1961 was a very important year in Agency history because "the Bay of Pigs essentially made CIA a public institution. Before then, the Agency was so secret that people didn't talk very much about it. After the Bay of Pigs, everything change[d]. All of a sudden there

[were] news stories, books [were] published, and investigative journalism flourishe[d]."[27]

Because the CIA first entered the public consciousness as a result of its failure in the Bay of Pigs operation[28] and the ensuing (failed) cover-up, it is unsurprising that the Agency has been cast as ineffective and untrustworthy. Intermittent news stories have subsequently reinforced this sentiment by highlighting serious CIA mistakes or seemingly inane plots. The CIA's efforts to assassinate Fidel Castro through an exploding cigar, its attempts to kill Patrice Lumumba with toxic toothpaste, and its reported accidental bombing of the Chinese embassy in Belgrade caused by its reliance on outdated maps are just a few examples that come to mind.[29]

Sometimes, though, the ineffective CIA operative is also used by filmmakers to make a more political statement, which is evidenced by the evolution of Felix Leiter, one of the first identified CIA officer characters to appear in film. While Leiter started out as a competent if bland sidekick in *Dr. No* (1962), his main role over the franchise's history is "to show just how superior the British are to the Americans."[30] In fact, Leiter is so bland and unmemorable that he has been played by nine actors, all of whom have played "second or third or fifth fiddle" to Bond.[31] These depictions of Leiter have ranged from a short, tubby bureaucrat to an African American operative who fails to bankrupt the villain Le Chiffre during a high-stakes card game in *Casino Royale* (2006) and thus must rely on 007 to save the day.

During the Pierce Brosnan movies, *GoldenEye* (1995) and *Tomorrow Never Dies* (1997), Leiter was replaced by Jack Wade, another inferior to Bond who reflects poorly on the Agency. Wade drives beat-up cars, sports excess weight and loud Hawaiian shirts, and is essentially the anti-Bond. In fact, Bruce Feirstein, a screenwriter for both movies, characterizes Wade as a "lunatic cowboy" distantly related to Robert Duvall's character in *Apocalypse Now*. He also argued that Wade's introduction to the franchise stemmed from the writers' desires to show how the CIA "was falling apart" in the mid-1990s, especially due to underfunding,[32] thus cementing the idea that art reflects, or at least interprets, history.

Positive Representations

Of course, not all films depicting the CIA have featured its officers so negatively. Some films have played up the spy genre's penchant for awesome gadgets and married them with the CIA's real strengths in technical intelligence. As a result, several films and television series have constructed the Agency as far ahead of the private sector technologically. Indeed, Hollywood's CIA has employed advanced disguises (e.g., *Mission: Impossible*), voice-imitation software, facial-recognition technology, microscopic bugs, advanced biometrics, and weaponry hidden in the unlikeliest of places. The Agency can also fake any document, replicate any object, track a person's every credit card purchase, and even follow someone across the globe in real time using nothing but satellite "zoom lenses." These elements undoubtedly depict the Agency in a positive light, and counter the image of the CIA as buffoonish or inept. (Although when its technological capacities are coupled with moral bankruptcy, they can work to make the CIA seem extremely dangerous and omnipresent.)

The Jack Ryan film series—*The Hunt for Red October* (1990), *Patriot Games* (1992), *Clear and Present Danger* (1994), and *The Sum of All Fears* (2002)—also depict the Agency in a relatively positive light. In *The Hunt for Red October*, Ryan, his boss, and the Agency are all cooperative and competent. This portrayal likewise continues in the next two installments, which feature Harrison Ford fighting Irish terrorists and Colombian drug lords as the deputy director of intelligence. Near the end of *Clear and Present Danger*, Ryan is even depicted as the government's moral compass, lecturing the president on the importance of operational oversight and the need to accept blame when negative consequences arise from covert action (although this film does depict a morally bankrupt, rogue officer, too). *The Sum of All Fears*, a CIA-Hollywood collaboration, is equally laudatory in its depictions of the Agency, as it features Ryan bravely jumping into the fray to help locate a nuclear bomb.

Other Contributors to the CIA's Negative Image

Despite the Jack Ryan films and other recent CIA-Hollywood collaborations, however, the depictions of a competent and moral CIA are rare. But is there anything else that may account for Hollywood's negative representations of the Agency besides its own history? The answer is yes. The demands of cinematic storytelling and the political leanings of Hollywood also play a crucial part.

More specifically, screenwriters and directors are asked to tell complicated stories in the space of just one to two hours, which pushes them to use highly recognizable archetypes to move a story forward at a fast pace. As such, espionage filmmakers have often relied on the negative images of the intelligence officer already established by spy novelists such as Graham Greene and John Le Carré. As a producer once explained to Chase Brandon, "if I am doing a movie where the CIA officer plays a bad guy, I can communicate that to viewers in just three words: 'rogue CIA agent.' Enough said. But if I want to do a film where the CIA officer is heroic, then it will take me ten pages of a script to communicate that. It is just a lot easier," the producer explained, "to cast the Agency as bad guys."[33]

In addition to the demands of visual storytelling, Bill Harlow argues that the very nature of Hollywood also encourages the negative representation of the CIA, since the entertainment industry is largely composed of liberals, who tend to view the intelligence community "with great suspicion."[34] "In general, they think the CIA is somehow harsh on civil liberties," he stated. "It takes a courageous Hollywood person to say something positive about the NSA or CIA because the default position in their social circles is to view the government and secret organizations with great skepticism."[35] In fact, Harlow argued that during his tenure, the most difficult task for the public affairs staff was to get people to make a movie in which the Agency's officers were the heroes or viewed in a positive light precisely because of the politics guiding the entertainment community.

This idea was also reinforced by the CIA entertainment liaison Paul Barry, who told me in 2008 that while the CIA's attrition rate remained low and application numbers continued to rise, the challenges "facing the public image of the CIA [were] more daunting" than right after 9/11. Part of this stemmed, he argued, from the strong opposition directed toward the Bush administration, which meant that films "were not being made about the positive contributions that the CIA [was] making; in fact, I've been told as much by those working in the entertainment industry," he added.

Of course, not everyone in Hollywood is left-leaning, but Harlow and Barry are right that many in the industry are critical of the intelligence community. To cite just one example, the American Civil Liberties Union launched a series of advertisements in 2003 that featured celebrities such as Al Pacino, Martin Sheen, Wendie Malick, Hector Elizondo, Richard Dreyfuss, Holly Hunter, Kristin Davis, Kurt Vonnegut, Samuel L. Jackson, and Jake Gyllenhaal beside text that was critical of the government and the intelligence community.[36] Kurt Vonnegut's ad read, "I am not an American who thinks my government should secretly get a list of the books I read. I am an American who knows the importance of being able to read and express any thought without fear." Holly Hunter's expressed a similar sentiment: "I am not an American who believes that questioning or criticizing my government is unpatriotic. I am an American whose voice and actions define who I am in a free society." These ads were released in response to the government's attempts to seize broader executive and surveillance powers in the aftermath of 9/11, and they support Barry and Harlow's point that the fiction and film community is often critical of the government and intelligence agencies, especially during more conservative administrations.

The CIA as a Victim of Hollywood?

Despite the political persuasion of many in Hollywood, the CIA is still not justified in painting itself as merely a victim of negative press. For one, the Agency's history shows that it has engaged in assassinations, evaded congressional oversight, and engaged in morally reprehensible activities over the years. Thus part of its negative image is deserved. Second, the CIA's lack of transparency, historical unwillingness to talk to the news media, and refusal to declassify older documents have also left the public, including those in Hollywood, to imagine the worst about what activities really take place inside the CIA.

Of course, part of the CIA's secrecy is necessary. As Harlow points out, many of the Agency's failures are publicly known but most of its successes are not: "It has to be that way if operatives want to use a particular strategy again, to protect the identities of its assets, and more."[37] Because the CIA cannot easily talk about its accomplishments, he continued, most of what Hollywood has to focus on are the CIA's screwups. The FBI, he stated, has long been known as a group of valiant crime busters more than sinister sneaks, partly because its officers can talk about what they do more easily.

But the CIA's secrecy goes beyond just operational protection to the point that it is sometimes laughable. For instance, when Robert Gates became the CIA's fifteenth director in 1991, one of his first acts was to create a task force to examine the Agency's openness policies, "in response to criticism that excessive secrecy had damaged its credibility and undermined its relations with Congress."[38] When the group finished its deliberations four weeks later, however, "the report was promptly classified, prompting a roar of collective laughter from reporters and editors around the country."[39] In another puzzling move, the CIA insisted in the late 1990s that it could "neither confirm nor deny" whether its classified archives included biographies on long-dead communist leaders — almost a decade after the collapse of the Berlin Wall.[40] And even I experienced the outfit's continued zealousness for secrecy during my research for this book. In early 2010, I called the CIA's PAO to ask who the director of public affairs was in the early 1990s. The woman on the other end of the line told me that the PAO did not release such names, which is ridiculous since the DPA is *the* public spokesperson for the Agency. (After my protests, she eventually called back to share that it was Kent Harrington.) This type of behavior runs deep throughout the CIA's history. In fact, until the late 1970s, James Grady claims that the CIA still answered their only listed phone number by saying "Hello."[41]

Such secrecy is dangerous for any intelligence community, because it leaves itself open to being seriously misunderstood. In the absence of real information about what intelligence services are doing, fantasists and conspiracy theorists are encouraged to use their imaginations. As Dujmovic explains, "Both types make things up in the absence of information and neither is based on reality."[42] Even Chase Brandon recognized the dangers of a closed community when he stated that the CIA's negative image in Hollywood partially stems from the fact that the Agency was never in the "position to respond to any writer who would have attempted to research" it in order to present a realistic image.[43] And screenwriters admit that in the absence of information regarding CIA activities, they fill in the gaps with outside research and invention.

Indeed, James Grady told me that he based his research for *Six Days of the Condor* "on the only three factual books about the CIA that were readily available" in the 1970s; the rest was based on hearsay and imagination.[44] Likewise, Peter Iliff, screenwriter of *Patriot Games*, notes that despite Tom Clancy's association with the project, the CIA provided "no help whatsoever" during the film's research process. Thus his team had to rely on books and comments made by former employees off the record to provide viewers with "our best guess as to what the CIA/NSA must have been capable of."[45]

The Impetus to Work with Hollywood

Until the CIA becomes more transparent, it cannot expect its image to change significantly; in the last twenty years, however, it has attempted to be more accessible to the Hollywood community. This initiative, launched in the early 1990s, was pitched to the public as a way for the Agency to correct misconceptions about the CIA and to reverse its image as a rogue, trigger-happy outfit. But this is only part of the story. To understand the other, hidden factors that led to the CIA's new relationship with Hollywood, one must trace the history of the Agency back to the collapse of the Soviet Union in 1991 and explore its first (failed) attempt to bolster its image, through a little-known television project called *The Classified Files of the CIA*. One must also examine the nature of more contemporary CIA relations to understand that the Agency is not interested in educating just anyone with a CIA-related project. Rather, it provides information and access to sympathetic producers but denies the same tools to those portraying the CIA in a negative light. Thus concerns of education and accuracy are secondary to the CIA. Its primary objective is to project a favorable image of itself in order to boost both its congressional and public support.

CHAPTER 2

Opening the Doors: Why and How the CIA Works with Hollywood

The CIA claims that it began cooperating with Hollywood in the 1990s to help reverse its image in film and television, since these mediums have usually depicted the Agency as a rogue, immoral outfit with a penchant for assassination and failure. Additionally, the CIA often frames its early cooperation efforts within the concepts of accuracy and education, stressing the danger of letting its negative image go unchecked. Indeed, Paul Barry claimed, "Hollywood is the only way that the public learns about the Agency."[1] Since most Americans "do not do their own research," he continued, "Hollywood's depictions of us become very important," especially as they shape the judgments Americans pass on the Agency's performance. As a result, Barry claimed that the CIA now works with Hollywood to increase the "accuracy" of its image and to inform the public about its role and activities.[2] Likewise, Chase Brandon argued that in the 1990s, the CIA finally realized that people were always going to make movies and TV series that featured the CIA, and "that if we didn't work with them, we were leaving ourselves open for misrepresentation. We have systematically been typecast as the bad guys in one movie after another," he said. "So we decided to help the industry portray the agency more accurately and fairly portray the CIA in scripts."[3]

The desire to ameliorate the Agency's negative image and to "educate" the public through motion pictures undoubtedly factored into the CIA's original decision to work with the industry. But these were not the only motives. The desire to reassure Americans about the need for intelligence in a post–Cold War world, to counter congressional accusations that the CIA had grown too secretive, and to conduct damage control in the wake of the Aldrich Ames case also played a major part. These factors belie the claim that the CIA is simply interested in educating the public through motion pictures; they illustrate that the Agency is also invested in Hollywood for its ability to boost both public and congressional support for the outfit, and to help the CIA mitigate public relations disasters. As a result, this chapter investigates each of these factors in detail and explains how they eventually led to the Agency's first major attempt at self-promotion through a tightly controlled television project called *The Classified Files of the CIA*. The chapter then goes on to illustrate how this show's failure to air encouraged the Agency to try a different approach to manipulating entertainment media by hiring its first entertainment industry liaison officer in 1996. It also explains how this new Agency initiative works with the Hollywood community in unique and surprising ways.

The Historical Factors That Led the CIA to Work with Hollywood in the 1990s

Within popular discourse, the CIA has long been accused of obsessing over secrecy, and not without reason. For example, employees of the CIA must sign a secrecy agreement as a condition of employment. This document makes it illegal for employees to disclose classified information or to publish any information obtained during one's tenure without the Agency's prior consent.[4] Writing in 1975, members of the *Yale Law Journal* also pointed to the "massive secrecy that envelops the CIA" when they challenged its practice of regularly refusing to disclose its annual budget, highlighting the fact that its funds are allocated by Congress through appropriations made through other government agencies.[5]

The CIA's reputation for secrecy is also reinforced by its (and the courts') interpretation of the Freedom of Information Act. This legislation is intended as a check on government agencies by legally requiring them to disclose documents pertaining to public policy when requested to do so by private citizens, journalists, and others. But the CIA has a near-blanket exemption from disclosing many of its files because of an exemption in the act, which states that no information is to be made public that could reasonably be expected to disclose the identity of a source who clearly expected and continues to expect that the source relationship will remain confidential. Information acquired by an agency conducting a lawful national security intelligence investigation is also exempt for at least twenty years. As Amy Rees notes in the *Duke Law Journal*, the CIA has repeatedly used this exemption to withhold information from inquiring citizens, regardless of whether the information poses a real national security risk.[6]

Because of this history of secrecy, many outsiders were surprised by the CIA's decision to open its doors to the entertainment industry in the 1990s. But the end of the Cold War and the significant demise of two of the United States' most prominent enemies—communism and the USSR—demanded a new paradigm. Indeed, after the 1989 destruction of the Berlin Wall and the 1991 collapse of the Soviet Union, many questioned whether the CIA would be necessary in the new age, and the Agency suffered from internal attrition. As Milt Bearden, the Soviet station chief during the Cold War, explains, "It was easy, once upon a time, for the CIA to be unique and mystical. It was not an institution. It was a mission. And the mission was a crusade. Then you took the Soviet Union away from us and there wasn't anything else."[7] In the absence of this mission, several officers soon left the Agency. Indeed, outside intelligence analysts believe that CIA employment levels dropped from twenty thousand near the end of the Cold War to sixteen thousand by 1997, a 20 percent staff reduction.[8] The United States' total budget for intelligence spending also decreased significantly during the decade. As the Federation of American Scientists illustrates, intelligence spending in 1990 had increased roughly 125 percent over the 1980 appropriation but fell to only an 80 percent increase over that same mark by 1996.[9]

Others also questioned the very need for the CIA in a post–Cold War world. During Robert Gates's confirmation hearings in 1991, for example, the CIA expert Harold Ford argued that the Agency had been "dead wrong" on the facts of life inside the Soviet Union, as the Agency continually claimed that the nation's economy was growing and expanding when in reality it was self-destructing.[10] Such accusations regarding the CIA's misjudgment, argues Tim Weiner, "called into question" the very "rationale for the Central Intelligence Agency"[11]—questions that lasted throughout most of the decade. Indeed, as late as November 1997, the Gerald R. Ford Library held an entire conference to debate the continued need for the CIA's existence.

Adding to the CIA's woes, in the early 1990s, Congress also began accusing numerous government agencies of being too secretive—accusations that culminated in Senator Daniel Patrick Moynihan's 1995 review of U.S. secrecy and classification practices. In its final report, Moynihan's Commission on Protecting and Reducing Government Secrecy concluded, "Excessive secrecy has significant consequences for the national interest when, as a result, policymakers are not fully informed, government is not held accountable for its actions, and the public cannot engage in informed debate."[12] The report also argued that the government's classification system "is used too often to deny the public an understanding of the policymaking process, rather than for the necessary protection of intelligence activities and other highly sensitive matters."[13] The CIA, largely renowned as one of the most secretive federal agencies, felt the weight of these words; not only was the necessity of the CIA's existence being questioned, but now it was also being accused of stymieing democracy and disserving the public interest.

In an early response to the convergence of these hostile forces, DCI Robert Gates created the Task Force for Greater CIA Openness in 1991. By his own account, Gates's goal was to garner "additional proposals for making more information about the Agency available to the American people and to give greater transparency to our organization."[14] The memorandums exchanged between the task force and Gates reveal that the CIA was indeed brainstorming ways to be more open, as evidenced by its suggestions to declassify documents and make available portions of its historical archives.

But the memorandums also reveal that the CIA faced a serious image problem and wanted to find more media-savvy ways of enhancing its public support under the same guise of "greater openness." One of the proposals put forth by the task force recognized the desperate need for a "visible spokesperson, such as the D/PAO, to refute [media] allegations and set the record straight. When such false allegations come from television, we need to be able to speak to them in the same forum" (the report then cited a 1991 episode of *Nightline* that criticized the CIA).[15] "An Agency spokesperson reading our statement in response to these allegations," it wrote, "would have been more effective than Ted Koppel's reading of it with raised eyebrows and a look of 'What do you expect given the source?'"[16]

The task force also argued that working with Hollywood could help the Agency with its public image. It explained that the PAO had already reviewed some "film scripts about the Agency at the request of filmmakers seeking guidance on accuracy and authenticity. In a few instances, we facilitated the filming of a few scenes on Agency premises. Responding positively to these requests in a limited way has provided PAO with the opportunity to help others depict the Agency and its activities accurately and without negative distortions."[17] In other words, by opening its doors to writers and filmmakers interested in researching the Agency, the CIA could claim it was making itself more open to the public, but by using its interactions with these groups to influence their portrayals of the CIA, it stood to gain a more favorable public image as well.

Despite this recognition, these memos indicate that the Agency did not seek to play a proactive role in filmmaking ventures in the late 1980s and early 1990s. For instance, although it knew that Oliver Stone's *JFK* was in the works for some time, the CIA "did not contact him to volunteer an Agency viewpoint," according to the memos.[18] This passive approach to the film industry was short-lived, however, and the event that finally pushed the CIA to work proactively with Hollywood was the 1994 case of the CIA officer turned traitor Aldrich Ames. Ames's betrayal forced the CIA to engage quickly and aggressively in a multi-platform strategy to mitigate the public fallout, which had dramatically added to the CIA's aforementioned woes. Part of this strategy entailed working with the motion picture industry in a full and proactive capacity, as evidenced by a little-known project called *The Classified Files of the CIA*.

Aldrich Ames and *The Classified Files of the CIA*

As explained in Pete Earley's *Confessions of a Spy*, Aldrich Ames was a CIA officer who eventually became the head of Soviet counterintelligence. In his attempt to clear a large personal debt, Ames sold the names of three Russian double agents to the KGB for $50,000 in 1985. Even though this sale paid off his debt, Ames continued his spying, eventually giving up the name of almost every Russian asset working for the CIA for a total of nearly $4.6 million. Many of these assets were quickly recalled to Moscow and shot or jailed. Within Langley, these assets became known as the "1985 losses" and sparked an almost eight-year investigation by a CIA-FBI joint task force to locate the mole. Because of a series of mishaps and Russian disinformation campaigns, it took the task force until the early part of 1994 to correctly identify and arrest Ames, who was finally charged with spying for the Soviet Union and sentenced to life in prison without parole.

Kent Harrington was the CIA's director of public affairs at the time of the Ames case. He argues that the Ames story was "devastating" to public perceptions of the Agency, as its inability to detect and prevent the officer's betrayal put Langley "in the bull's eye for its failures."[19] Also damaging to the Agency was Ames's own testimony, as he claimed that the whole espionage business was a "self-serving sham, carried out by careerist bureaucrats who have managed to deceive several generations of American policy makers and the public about both the necessity and the value of their work."[20] Ames claimed that there is "no rational need for thousands of case officers and tens of thousands of agents working around the world, . . . as the information our vast espionage network acquires is generally insignificant or irrelevant to our policy makers' needs."[21]

Ames's remarks, in conjunction with the CIA's decreasing prominence in the post–Cold War era, led politicians to consider further the necessity of the Agency. For instance, Rep. Dan Glickman, who headed the House intelligence committee, publicly questioned whether counterintelligence makes "any difference at all" in the modern world, while Senator Moynihan even suggested abolishing the CIA altogether and assigning its duties to intelligence departments in other agencies.[22] While Harrington feels that Moynihan's comments were more "symbolic than substantive," he notes that the Ames case was an "especially significant blow" because it intersected with the growing public perception that the CIA was no longer needed. In this "era of the 'peace dividend' and other illusions," he stated, "there was already a conversation circulating in Washington as to whether or not we needed intelligence gathering anymore. . . . The CIA's failure regarding Ames only made things worse."[23]

Indeed, the damage caused by Ames would prove to be the most significant factor that led the CIA to invest fully in Hollywood, causing Harrington to embark on a new public relations strategy. According to Harrington, his job during the first three months of his tenure was to keep Director James Woolsey out of the press's reach (so much for openness). "But events changed when Aldrich Ames happened," he stated.[24] Because the PAO had to be ready to deal with the case's public and congressional consequences, Harrington looked to develop a multifaceted strategy to address the crisis: "I had to seek to put Jim in positions where he could better tell the story of the Agency and how it was trying to fix the problems that Ames revealed about counterintelligence and the Soviet penetration of the CIA. . . . Sometimes that meant putting Woolsey on TV, but it also meant reaching out to the public [through the entertainment industry] about the CIA and the nature of its business in the post–Cold War era."[25]

As part of this multi-platform initiative, Harrington and Woolsey quickly began developing *The Classified Files of the CIA*, which was envisioned as a weekly dramatic television series. Actual case files were to serve as the basis for episode content, and the show itself was heavily modeled on the 1960s anthology series *The F.B.I.* This earlier series, often regarded as a blatant propaganda campaign launched under J. Edgar Hoover's administration, ran on ABC from 1965 to 1974 during prime family-viewing hours. It opened and closed every episode with the FBI seal, and crawl credits thanked Hoover and his associates for their cooperation in the program's production.

In a *TV Guide* article published shortly after his death, Hoover wrote that he passed on nearly six hundred offers to make an FBI television series before agreeing to work with two men he knew he could trust: Jack Warner of Warner Bros., who had made *G-Men* (1935), and James Hagerty, president of ABC, whom Hoover came to know when Haggerty served as President Eisenhower's press secretary.[26] By his own admission, Hoover demanded complete control over scripts, sponsorships, and personnel, and internal memos reveal that Milton A. Jones, the FBI section chief who oversaw the TV series's daily operations, never allowed "drunkards, kooks, perverts, faggots, junkies and others of this ilk" to work on the show, including, "people like Jane Fonda and Dalton Trumbo of the Hollywood Ten."[27] According to Richard Powers, the Bureau's revisions to scripts showed "keen attention to any adverse implications, no matter how farfetched, on the FBI's reputation for decorum, thoroughness and precision."[28]

Such control led *The F.B.I.* to present "an unvaryingly upbeat—and largely distorted—portrait of a supremely ethical, non-politicized institution," which, according to Jeff Cohen, was part of Hoover's efforts to "polish the bureau's image in the mass media as a means toward more power and more funding."[29] Hoover's strategy may have worked: forty million Americans watched the program each week and the series ran in more than fifty countries, helping to sell the wholesome image of the FBI's G-men worldwide[30] and to encourage many young boys to consider a career in the FBI.

The Agency's work on *The Classified Files of the CIA* mirrored Hoover's project in many ways. For instance, while numerous groups had asked to produce a show for the Agency in the past, the CIA, like the FBI, chose a team that it could trust to protect its interests—Jack Myers and David Houle, cofounders of Television Production Partners (TPP). As Myers explained, the CIA was highly aware of TPP's interest in doing projects "that were supportive of America and American life."[31] Our positive approach to content meant that we "wouldn't tear down American culture or society, and that resonated with the CIA. . . . We never promised to be a mouthpiece for [them], but that having been said, the nature of the program would've been to present . . . their stories and the roles they played globally"[32] in a positive light.

Additionally, TPP's economic structure interested the CIA, as the company in the early 1990s had begun putting together a consortium of U.S. advertisers willing to sponsor its programming. "It was a system akin to the 1950s when a single sponsor paid for a program," Houle stated, "only we were working with a group of advertisers in the way that television shows often do now"[33] (e.g., *American Idol*). Those companies included General Motors, Coca-Cola, MasterCard, Coors, Campbell's, and Clorox, which Houle referred to as "America's brands." As the CIA was essentially looking to recast its image in the post-Cold War era, Houle claimed, "Who could be better than [us] to re-brand a fundamental American organization?"[34]

TPP further demonstrated its desire and ability to depict the Agency in a positive light through its hiring practices. For instance, Houle recalled that Steve Tisch was brought on to produce the show right after he won an Academy Award for his work on *Forrest Gump* in order to make the series more attractive to the studios.[35] Even though Tisch was a well-respected producer and wanted to do the series, many of the proposed writers and directors had trouble with the show's concept—either because they saw it as controlled by the Agency or because they held negative opinions of the CIA.[36] As such, these individuals were not selected for the project. Houle also noted that he personally felt a "need to protect the CIA's rights on the project," joking:

> It's ironic because I came of age in the sixties, when the CIA was the
> bad guy. When I went there for my first meeting, I remember thinking,
> "Great, here's where all of those photos of me marching in Washing-
> ton protests have ended up." But when I went there and started meeting
> with people, I realized that the CIA was just made up of individuals who
> weren't very James Bond–like at all. They simply had a job that often re-
> quired them to keep secrets. These guys had families in the suburbs, and
> I found I really liked the actual people who did the job; they were com-
> mitted, hardworking people. I felt protective of them and their mission
> [especially since] Hollywood was very derisive of them.[37]

Later memos written during Dennis Boxx's term as director of public affairs reinforce the idea that TPP was selected for the project due to its interest in developing programming that "portrays American institutions in a positive light"[38] (see figure 2.2). But the CIA also selected TPP for the "extraordinary" amount of control it would afford the Agency during the preproduction and production process.[39] For instance, like the producers (b)(3)   03 October 1995

MEMORANDUM FOR: Dennis Boxx
                     Vin Swasev

FROM:

SUBJECT: CIA Television Series Project

     1.   During the week of 18 September, Jack Myers and David
Houle of Television Production Partners (TPP) met in Los Angeles
with representatives of 20th Century Fox Television to discuss a
possible agreement on the proposed CIA television series.   TPP
characterized these meetings as positive and productive.   TPP and
20th Century Fox Television agreed to begin discussions focusing
on the business aspects of their potential relationship.   20th
Century Fox Television also identified a number of issues
contained in the original CIA-TPP Letter of Agreement that needed
to be resolved prior to establishing a production agreement.   TPP
has provided CIA with these concerns as well as their
recommendations on each point.

     2.   I have conducted a paragraph by paragraph comparison of
the Agency's original agreement with TPP, 20th Century Fox
Television's concerns, and TPP's recommendations.   The details of
this comparison and recommendations for further action are
attached.   Overall, I identified:

     -    four issues that are primarily business or legal in
nature and may be readily resolved following OGC review
(transferability, production rights, copyright and distribution
rights, CIA reproduction rights);
     -    two issues that CIA may wish to amend to address
production concerns (use of the term "docudrama" and contract
renewal provisions);
     -    one significant issue that CIA may wish to use as a
negotiating point (use of the CIA name and seal); and,
     -    a minimum of six issues that constitute either
significant departures from project discussions to date or
fundamental areas needing clarification or resolution.

These last issues primarily focus on the extent of
fictionalization, the use of non-CIA material, acknowledgment of
CIA cooperation, and CIA's script review and approval.

of *The F.B.I.*, TPP agreed to base episodes on actual case files provided by
the Agency. It also agreed to work with a retired officer named Warren,
who had become an unofficial archivist within the Agency.[40] Warren was
meant to act as the official conduit between the CIA and TPP, identifying files that could eventually be turned into scripts. TPP was allowed to
embellish the case summaries for dramatic purposes so long as they were

3. These six or more issues, taken as a whole, apparently indicate a shift from the agreed series concept -- a dramatic television series based exclusively on synopses taken from actual CIA files with significant attention given to CIA's cooperation in the production -- to a more traditional production format in which CIA synopses and other information may or may not be used in conjunction with other fictional material to produce each episode and the importance of CIA's cooperation is diminished. This shift is not surprising as it is consistent with the obstacles TPP has encountered in their discussions with Steve Tisch and Aaron Spelling. TPP's initial agreement with CIA affords the Agency much greater control than what appears to be the industry norm and the concerns raised represent attempts to bring this agreement back into line with accepted industry practices. It is unlikely that CIA would have agreed to these requirements if they had been presented during the initial discussions.

4. Given the apparent shift in the focus of this project, the fundamental question now facing the Agency is whether the possible benefits derived from our continued cooperation in this project outweigh the concessions, loss of control, and resources that will be required to support it. The Agency's role, as it appears to be taking shape, seems to be little more than a possible source of story material and an occasional technical advisor. Such a role is consistent with the support provided to the entertainment industry by many other Government agencies and may still merit consideration. It may still represent a means to work with the entertainment media to provide a more realistic and fair portrayal of CIA but it is not what was originally agreed to by PAS, the EXCOM, the DDCI and DCI.

Attachments

A - Comparison Between Original CIA-TPP
    Letter of Agreement and Concerns Identified by 20th Century
    Fox Television
B - CIA-TPP Letter of Agreement
C - 20th Century Fox Television Internal Memorandum
D - TPP Correspondence to DD/PAS

Fig. 2.1. 1995 "CIA Television Series Project" memo. Available through the CIA's Electronic Reading Room at http://www.foia.cia.gov/.

"consistent with US laws and general CIA practices,"[41] and TPP had even considered hiring two former senior Agency officials to serve as technical advisers to help with this element of the project.

More notably, TPP also granted the CIA the right to approve all scripts in advance of production, in exchange for the use of the Agency's seal and the acknowledgment that the program's stories were based on actual CIA files. If the CIA did not want to approve a specific script, TPP could either revise it to address CIA concerns, or air the episode without the use of the CIA's name and seal. That episode would also need to feature (b)(3)

16 April 96
PAS-96-0066

MEMORANDUM FOR: Executive Director

FROM: Dennis R. Boxx
                     Director of Public Affairs

SUBJECT: CIA Television Series

       The PAS project to collaborate in the production of a television series based on unclassified CIA file summaries has progressed to the point where it is appropriate to review our commitments and the steps that will be required to ensure the project's success. A planning meeting with the production company, Television Production Partners (TPP), is scheduled for 25 April. I would like to discuss this project with you at the earliest convenience.

       Background: The intent of this project, initiated by DCI Woolsey in the spring of 1994, is to expand our use of the entertainment media to promote a realistic and positive public image of CIA and intelligence, to dispel a number of intelligence myths and misperceptions commonly promoted by the entertainment industry, and to support a popular project that would benefit employee morale. TPP was selected as the production company for this project based on its stated interest in developing programming that portrays American institutions in a positive light and due to the extraordinary control it would allow CIA in reviewing the production. This project was briefed to and approved by the CIA EXCOM in December 1994 and a Letter of Agreement between CIA and TPP was signed by Acting DCI Studeman at the end of that month. TPP has recently concluded an agreement with 20th Century Fox Television for the production of a two hour television movie that will serve as the pilot for a potential weekly dramatic series.

       Commitments: CIA has agreed to provide TPP with unclassified summaries drawn from actual CIA files that will serve as the bases for story and script development. TPP is authorized to embellish these summaries for dramatic purposes provided the resulting depictions are consistent with US laws and general CIA practices. TPP is considering hiring two former senior Agency officials to serve as technical advisors to review this aspect of the story development. CIA will review and approve or deny all stories and scripts produced. In exchange for this extraordinary control, CIA has granted TPP the right to use the CIA name and seal in the production and to state that the stories are fictional accounts based on actual CIA files. In the event that CIA does not approve a specific script, TPP may either revise the script to address CIA concerns or air the episode without use of the CIA name and seal and include a disclaimer that the episode was not produced with the cooperation of CIA.

       Potential: This project presents an unprecedented opportunity for CIA to influence the portrayal of this Agency and US intelligence in a potentially high profile and successful television series reaching millions of Americans. It has been briefed to and has the support of both congressional oversight committees. The extent of CIA control and the commitment of TPP to develop a realistic and positive depiction of CIA greatly increases the likelihood of an acceptable production as compared to previous entertainment projects in which we have cooperated.

Issues: Efforts over the last two years have focused on structuring an agreement that will ensure protection of CIA equities while also allowing flexibility for creative development. Now that TPP has reached an agreement with a major network, there are a number of issues that must be addressed as the project proceeds toward production. These issues include:

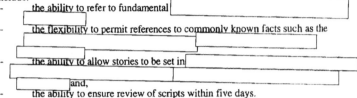

- the ability to refer to fundamental
- the flexibility to permit references to commonly known facts such as the
- the ability to allow stories to be set in

  and,
- the ability to ensure review of scripts within five days.

Furthermore, if the initial two hour pilot is a success and leads to production of a weekly series, we must be in a position to ensure a continuing supply of unclassified synopses incorporating various operational, analytical, administrative, technical, and human interest aspects of the Agency.

Review Process: Throughout the project, PAS must be able to operate with confidence that the information provided and cooperation rendered is consistent with existing CIA policies, procedures, and legal precedents, specifically in the area of official acknowledgments and FOIA decisions. I believe this will require the creation of a small TPP project review body that will have the authority to consider and approve both the unclassified synopses and the resulting scripts. This body must also be able to conduct these reviews within the five day period agreed to with TPP. The proposed review body may include an Associate Deputy Director from each directorate as well as the General Counsel and the Director of Public Affairs.

I would like to discuss this project as soon as possible, perhaps at the next Seniors Meeting, and review the anticipated issues and requirements the project entails. The project is now at a critical stage where CIA management must be in agreement regarding our commitments and flexibility if we are to proceed with development and production.

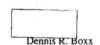

Dennis R. Boxx

Fig. 2.2. 1996 "CIA Television Series" memo. Available through the CIA's Electronic Reading Room at http://www.foia.cia.gov/.

a disclaimer stating that it was not produced with the cooperation of the Agency.[42] Myers argues that this arrangement did not mean that the CIA "got to write the scripts or change the truth, it just meant that they had the right to review and veto something that was not accurate, in the national interest, or contrary to how they perceived the role of the CIA to actually be."[43] Myers also believes that TPP was actually given more creative freedoms than most production companies working with government agencies, as it had the right to continue with an episode even if the CIA objected to something in the script.[44]

While Myers' point is well taken, the CIA's arrangements with TPP meant that the Agency nonetheless exerted very strong control over the program's content. For instance, script material was to be culled from the CIA's case files, but it was the Agency archivist who would select them. It is likely that he would have first sanitized the files delivered, and before that, selected only cases that avoided controversial subject matter and highlighted CIA successes. After all, the show's purpose stemmed from the Agency's need to temper criticism directed at the CIA after the Ames case became public knowledge. It is also unlikely that TPP could have regularly disagreed with the CIA to the point of the Agency revoking its endorsement, given that the premise and marketing strategy of the series rested on its official ties to the outfit. As with *The F.B.I.*, the show's writers would probably not have raised any complicated or controversial questions regarding the CIA's activities either, given their very dependence on the Agency for source material and branding. Thus, while the CIA was not going to be able to "write the scripts," it was going to possess an extraordinary amount of creative control over the final product.

Precisely because of the concessions TPP was willing to afford the CIA, the Agency's PAO praised *The Classified Files of the CIA* for its "unprecedented opportunity" to influence the portrayal of the Agency in a "potentially high profile and successful television series reaching millions of Americans."[45] But problems began to arise as the series neared closer to production. Agency memos indicate that Steve Tisch and possibly Aaron Spelling[46] began resisting CIA controls in the final stages of negotiations. In a memo dated October 1995, an anonymous author in the CIA's PAO lamented that recent developments reflected a shift away from the program's initial concept[47] (see figure 2.1). Originally, the officer stated, the project was envisioned as a dramatic series "based exclusively on synopses taken from actual CIA files with significant attention given to CIA's cooperation in the production." Near the end of 1995, however, the program looked more like a "traditional production format in which

CIA synopses . . . may or may not be used in conjunction with other fictional material," and where "the importance of CIA's cooperation is diminished."[48]

The memo claims that this "shift is not surprising," given that TPP's initial agreement afforded the Agency greater control than the industry norm and that Tisch and Spelling wished to bring those controls back within industry standards. As Houle further explained, when "we moved into the contract phase, the network, as always, insisted on final creative control."[49] It wanted greater options to make changes to scripts and "to secure the rights to the final product. . . . The CIA had problems with this."[50] Nonetheless, the program moved ahead, probably because the Agency still saw value in the project despite its diminished control. In fact, Dennis Boxx reported in early 1996 that the project had been presented to both congressional oversight committees, and both supported the endeavor. He also recommended that the CIA create a small project review body to approve both the unclassified synopses on which the show would be based, and the resulting scripts themselves.[51] By April of that same year, the series had been sold to Twentieth Century Fox, which began work on a two-hour television movie to serve as the pilot.

But still the program never aired. As Myers explained, The Classified Files of the CIA was first developed in 1994 under DCI Woolsey. Because of the Ames case, the CIA was especially supportive of the series, as Woolsey recognized the need "to have a more friendly, open communication with the American public about the CIA."[52] But Woolsey exited the CIA in 1995 and was replaced by John Deutch. According to Myers, Deutch did not value "public outreach," and thus during his tenure he instructed the CIA to shut down a number of outreach initiatives—The Classified Files of the CIA among them. "I have no doubt that if DCI Woolsey had still been at the helm of the CIA [in 1996]," Myers stated, "our program would've made it onto the air, especially since we already had a signed contract with Twentieth Century Fox and Steve Tisch had agreed to produce it."[53] Houle admitted that the series' cancellation was extremely disappointing: "We were the first company to work with the CIA at high levels and have their support to bring a treasure trove of material to Hollywood. We came so close to creating a breakthrough series and an opportunity for the CIA to burnish its reputation."[54] He also added that the cancellation continued to be hard to digest in the years that followed, since the CIA went on to support several projects that depicted the Agency in less "realistic" ways and gave the Agency even less creative control than what TPP had agreed to.

So what does the story of *The Classified Files of the CIA* teach us, despite the fact that the show never made it to air? For one, the project belies the CIA's claims that it is simply interested in reversing the negative Agency images that Hollywood perpetuates, as it attempted to use this series to mitigate a public relations disaster and to generate interest in the Agency in the post–Cold War era. In fact, Houle recalls that *The Classified Files of the CIA* was largely envisioned as a recruitment tool, not just as a way to help the CIA get past the Ames debacle. He specifically recalled that the CIA was very fond of the film *Top Gun* (1986): "That film, they said, was the single best recruiting tool the navy—and specifically naval aviation—ever had, as applications and recruits skyrocketed after the film was released." The CIA "was looking for a project that could help them do something similar," Houle stated, which is part of the reason why TPP got the call in 1994 to discuss the development of a series.

Second, the project complicates the CIA's claims that it is interested in educating the public through its work with Hollywood. For instance, Kent Harrington argues that after Ames, the CIA was invested in showing the Agency "as it actually existed"; thus it was excited by the TPP project since Jack Myers wanted to do something that was factually based, along the lines of *The F.B.I.*[55] "The core of my reaction to this show was positive," Harrington continued, "because Jack wanted to do something that would be capable of educating the broad public about the role of intelligence, which is rarely shown in the whole proliferation of films that feature the Agency."[56]

While the series would have likely counterbalanced the image of the CIA officer as a rogue assassin engaged in James Bond foolery, it would have still only educated viewers about the CIA's successes and presented a highly sanitized version of the Agency. In other words, it would have served as government propaganda more than government education, which should encourage viewers to think critically about the Agency by painting a complete and nuanced picture. Unsurprisingly, this same criticism was often launched at *The F.B.I.*; in fact, when it went off the air in 1974, congressional hearings and Freedom of Information Act lawsuits soon revealed that during the show's nine-year run, "the bureau was systematically abusing the First Amendment rights of countless civil rights and peace advocates, from grass-roots activists to John Lennon and Martin Luther King Jr."[57] The show, however, only depicted a wholesome, do-good image of the Bureau, and thus masked these incongruities in the public domain.[58]

Finally, while Houle, Myers, Harrington, and Woolsey were all supportive of *The Classified Files of the CIA* and championed Langley's creative controls, Tisch, Spelling, and Fox were uncomfortable with the arrangement and worked to reclaim some creative freedoms in order to ensure a profitable venture. Indeed, television's basic economic structure suggests that networks and producers, even if they are supportive of the government, still want the final say about what is actually aired in order to protect their investments and advertisers. Another lesson this project teaches us, then, is that tightly controlled government projects are very difficult to produce in the modern motion picture industry, even with sympathetic creators. In other words, without outside pressures, like McCarthy's blacklists, industry creators have little incentive to give up such large amounts of creative control to the government. History indicates that the Agency learned this lesson well, as it did not attempt to repeat another such project again. Instead, the CIA chose a different tactic to bolster its image in Hollywood when it hired its first entertainment liaison in 1996.

The CIA and Hollywood: The Role of the Entertainment Liaison

While Myers and Houle believe that Director Deutch cancelled *The Classified Files of the CIA* in 1996 because he did not value public outreach, it is not clear that this is entirely the case. In that same year the CIA hired its first entertainment industry liaison officer—a twenty-five-year Agency veteran named Chase Brandon—to help the Agency more effectively work with Hollywood.[59] According to Bill Harlow, George Tenet's director of public affairs, Brandon was selected for the position because he was the first cousin of Tommy Lee Jones, which meant that he was able to come into the job with numerous Hollywood contacts already in place. Additionally, Brandon was "an engaging, loquacious guy" and a "free spirit" who used to trek around in the jungles of Central America, so "the Hollywood-types loved him."[60] All these attributes, Harlow argued, made Brandon well suited for the job, and indeed, the liaison would serve in his position for eleven years, working under four different CIA directors, until his retirement in 2007.

According to Harlow, the decision to work with Hollywood through an entertainment liaison program "made a lot of sense" and was partially the result of his and Dennis Boxx's background.[61] (Boxx served as Director Deutch's DPA and was there when Brandon was originally hired.) Before joining the CIA, Harlow served as a navy public affairs officer, and

Boxx served the Pentagon as a civilian public affairs specialist. As the military has long understood the benefits of working with Hollywood to increase levels of recruitment and public support, Harlow suggested that he and Boxx also saw the benefits that a similar program might reap for the CIA and therefore supported its development.

In fact, the CIA's entertainment liaison program is modeled after the Pentagon's, as both programs' liaisons work with film and television companies to provide them with advice, technical consultants, shooting locations, props, and equipment when they seek to make movies involving their agency. Before granting access to such resources, however, these liaisons will request to see the project's script to ensure that it depicts their agency in a positive light; if it does not, they will either refuse to assist the project or negotiate their assets to secure a more positive representation.

For instance, when I asked Paul Barry (Brandon's successor) to walk me through the CIA's process of responding to requests for assistance from filmmakers, he stated that initial discussions gravitate toward the project's focus and requirements. If the industry representative is seeking assistance outside the realm of advice or guidance, the next step is to review the script, just like at the Pentagon. During this stage, Barry stated that he is specifically looking for a project directly connected to the CIA's strategic intent, especially its elements of service, integrity, excellence, and mission to "recruit, develop and retain exceptional individuals from a diverse talent pool."[62] Barry also stated that while there are no written guidelines that he follows, ultimately he is looking for projects that will increase understanding of the Agency and instill pride in its employees. "My guiding principles for cooperation," he added, "generally require that the project represents an authentic portrayal of the organization, seeks to provide a favorable impression of the organization, and suggests that there is a reasonable expectation that the project will stimulate positive interest in the organization."[63] Films that do not meet these requirements are asked to make a set of requested changes or are simply not granted assistance from the CIA.

By its own admission, however, the CIA, unlike the Pentagon, is unable to exert strong influence over projects that have reached the production stage, since it does not have the expensive equipment to offer film crews in return for script control. For instance, Phil Strub, the Pentagon's special assistant to the media, often provides military personnel and equipment, including fighter jets, submarines, and aircraft carriers at little to no cost to film and television creators as long as they seek to make movies that depict the military in a positive light. Strub also leverages access to the DOD's equipment to get entertainment professionals to change facts, dialogue, and scenes according to military discretion. "Phil Strub can actually say, 'I want pages six and seven completely thrown out or you don't get to use our aircraft carrier,'" Brandon stated.[64] "We can't do that," because the only thing the CIA can really barter with is its access to technical consultants and to CIA headquarters for filming.[65] The Agency can also leverage permission to use its official seal, which is protected under the 1947 National Security Act. "But the reality," states Barry, "is that it is easier and less expensive for Hollywood to simply recreate a facsimile of our lobby elsewhere" for the spy genre's "money shot."[66]

This difference in bargaining power is key to understanding the uniqueness of CIA-Hollywood collaborations, because it means that Langley is most effective in influencing story lines in the preproduction stage, when it can suggest ideas as they are being crafted. This sentiment is reflected in Barry's assertion that the CIA is most valuable when it works to offer advice to screenwriters when a film or program is in its early stages.[67] "From my experience," he said, "We can be a tremendous asset to writers developing characters and storylines." But "once a story has been optioned for a movie, it's almost too late for us to participate."[68] What Barry really means, however, is that once a story has been optioned, it is very difficult for the CIA to effectively negotiate with the producers to ensure the Agency's positive portrayal.

So how has the CIA worked to influence texts in the preproduction stage? For one, Barry scoured trade journals such as the *Hollywood Reporter* and *Variety* and then contacted the producers of relevant upcoming projects to let them know about his services.[69] On the entertainment liaison's webpage, Barry also created a space called "Now Playing," which suggests possible story lines for writers and producers to explore. Of course, these suggestions only feature CIA successes, including the engineering of the Berlin Tunnel, the story of "a potent counterintelligence response" against the East called "The Farewell Dossier," and the Agency's "superb" efforts regarding air operations in Laos from 1955 to 1974.[70]

Harlow recalls that Brandon, who worked twenty feet away from him, also spent "countless" hours on the phone pitching ideas to writers and working with directors.[71] He also traveled to Los Angeles roughly once a month to "make the rounds" and establish new contacts.[72] At one stage, the CIA even hired Michael Sands, a defense contractor, actor, and media image consultant, to further its network of Hollywood contacts. Starting in 2007, Sands began introducing Barry to people such as Scott Valentine, vice president of Sony Pictures; Jack Gilardi, executive vice president at

International Creative Management; Rick Nicita, partner at Creative Artists Agency; Ron Meyer, president and COO of Universal Studios; and several others.[73] According to Sands, Barry was particularly interested in meeting with Nicita because his wife, Paula Wagner, was the copresident of Cruise/Wagner Productions. At the time, Tom Cruise intended to play the lead role in *Salt*, a CIA operative accused of being a Russian sleeper. His company was in the process of rewriting the film script, and thus Barry wanted to offer his assistance.[74] Sands also noted that he and Barry recruited the actress Kristy Swanson (who starred in the 1992 film *Buffy the Vampire Slayer*) to work for the CIA in an overt capacity to help introduce Barry to more industry executives.[75]

CIA directors also assist the Agency. For instance, Director Tenet was the keynote speaker at the annual Sun Valley meetings in Idaho in 2003 and again in 2005.[76] Sun Valley draws together several hundred of the biggest names in American media, including most major Hollywood studio executives. The purpose of the meetings is to discuss collective media strategy for the coming year. As Matthew Alford and Robbie Graham write, "Against the idyllic backdrop of expansive golf courses, pine forests and clear fishing lakes, deals are struck, contracts are signed, and the face of the American media is quietly altered."[77] The press has minimal access to the event, which makes Sun Valley comparable to the annual Bilderberg conference, where influential people from the fields of politics, banking, business, the military, and the media come together to discuss global issues behind closed doors.[78]

Through each of these efforts, the CIA has successfully managed to inform the motion picture industry about its services, and now television and film creators initiate contact with the Agency as well. Such was the case for Matt Corman and Chris Ord, the creators of the USA Network's *Covert Affairs*, which debuted in 2010. In late 2007, Corman and Ord worked to contact Paul Barry through a combination of the CIA's liaison webpage and contacts they had already established while working on a film about the Senate. Because *Covert Affairs* is largely set within the confines of CIA headquarters and features a CIA field officer named Annie Walker, the two sought the Agency's advice during the research and writing stage since, as Corman states, "our entire conception of the CIA was based on other TV shows and movies, so we wanted to form our own opinions."[79]

Corman and Ord state that the CIA public affairs team was reluctant to assist the pair at first, and before offering them assistance asked to see several drafts of the show's scripts to ensure that the program would depict the Agency in a positive light. Because it was never "our intent to smear the CIA," we felt comfortable doing that, says Corman, who argues that once the CIA understood that the pair's primary intentions were to explore the CIA as a workplace, "they became more comfortable with us coming to ask a lot of questions"[80] and eventually opened their doors to the producers. For instance, Corman, Ord, and Piper Perabo, the lead actress in the series, were eventually invited to tour the campus and meet with the CIA media relations staff. Perabo also got to visit an operations center and meet with several female officers to get a better understanding of her character. Because Annie Walker has a language background, the producers also interviewed via conference call a linguist working in the field. "We would ask questions to this guy, who said his name was Massoud," said Corman. At times, the CIA liaisons "would take us off speaker phone to discuss how he could/should answer the questions, and then he would come back on. So it was sort of a filtered conversation, but it was really helpful to us because we understood what he does, some of the problems that he faces. He was just extremely helpful."

Corman and Ord also noted that after Barry's retirement in 2008, they have continued to work with the CIA's media relations team, primarily though George Little. The creators specifically said that they often call Little to ask questions to gather research data, and that overall, this information helps shape "the writing, the lingo, and the set design" of the show. Their interactions with the CIA also help the pair understand what life is like for those working inside the Agency—from larger philosophical questions to more minute details, like the fact that there's a Starbucks inside the campus and that the CIA hosts singles mixers to encourage intra-Agency dating. The CIA also supplies them with HD stock footage of the campus from different angles.

Corman and Ord are quick to argue that their show—which attracted roughly five million viewers per episode during its first season and ranked as the highest-rated scripted cable premiere among eighteen-to-forty-nine-year-olds in 2010[81]—"is not propaganda." Their relationship with the CIA is "loose," and by loose, Ord means, "We're not paying them, and they are not flying out here to visit specifically with us. It's a casual arrangement, a nice exchange of ideas. We ask for advice and bounce ideas off of them, but this is not propaganda. At the end of the day, we want to maintain our creative controls. We would never [be] beholden . . . to them in a way that would limit that."[82] Ord also points out that in their show, "the CIA is portrayed as having problems and leaks, and all sorts of personalities, you know, some Machiavellian types," which they argue the CIA thinks is "interesting and somewhat appropriate."[83]

Interestingly, however, the show's season finale, which aired in September 2010, clearly suggests that the CIA's leak does not actually stem from within the Agency. Instead, it comes from Henry Wilcox, the former director of the National Clandestine Service, whom the CIA ousted. Was this narrative decision the result of Corman and Ord trying to stay in the CIA's good graces by placing the source outside the Agency, or were other industry and creative factors at play?

The truth is that it is almost impossible for outsiders to know exactly how the CIA is able to influence the content of programs or creators' attitudes toward the Agency: no documentation has surfaced regarding the CIA's notes on creators' originally submitted drafts, and presumably, no recorded conversations between these players exist. The process of influence is also subtle and psychologically complicated, making it very difficult for even creators, let alone outsiders, to understand how the CIA may have influenced a text. It is clear, though, that by working with the CIA during their research process, Corman and Ord's ideas about the Agency were undoubtedly shaped by its media relations team, whose very job is to portray the Agency in a positive light. It is also clear that in order to gain and ultimately continue their relationship with the CIA, the creators of *Covert Affairs* need to present the Agency in a mostly favorable manner.[84] So while their relationship is fairly characterized as "loose," this does not mean the CIA is not trying to influence popular media creators to circulate a more favorable image of itself, or that the Agency's attempts do not constitute government propaganda.

As this case study demonstrates, the CIA no longer works with the entertainment industry in a tightly controlled manner, as it did when *The Classified Files of the CIA* was in development. Instead, it now tries to work with creators in the preproduction stages to influence ideas as they are being crafted, and this makes much of the CIA's work with Hollywood very difficult for industry outsiders to trace or fully understand. This difficulty is also augmented by the fact that the CIA has not released any documents detailing their specific correspondence with filmmakers or its influence over scripts, even though other government agencies have released similar documents.[85] Likewise, CIA public affairs officers are rarely credited in sources like the Internet Movie Database or on a program's scrolling credits, making it hard for viewers even to identify which texts have a CIA influence unless the media decides to report on it.

In many ways, this model of secret influence is similar to how the CIA worked with the news media in the 1960s and 1970s. In his *Rolling Stone* exposé, Carl Bernstein explains how the CIA enlisted the help of dozens of newspaper columnists and commentators to publish stories that were sympathetic to the Agency's viewpoint (and sometimes written by the Agency itself). Bernstein reveals that most of the CIA's use of the news media was orchestrated by high-level officials personally dealing "with a single designated individual in the top management of the cooperating news organization,"[86] making its relationship very hard to trace by outside researchers.

But the CIA's lack of transparency does not mean that *nothing* is known about its involvement or that trends cannot be discerned by analyzing its texts. Indeed, the next two chapters are devoted to explaining what I've learned about the CIA's work in Hollywood in recent years, starting with its first major collaborations that made it to viewers: *In the Company of Spies* and *The Agency*.

CHAPTER 3

Necessary and Competent: The CIA in *The Agency* and *In the Company of Spies*

While *The Classified Files of the CIA* never made it to viewers, other CIA-assisted projects began to appear by the turn of the millennium. These texts were not as tightly controlled by the Agency, which had recruited its own production company, provided the source material, and secured script-review rights for the joint CIA-TPP project. Rather, these new collaborations focused on an entertainment liaison assisting outside creators in the preproduction and production stages in order to shape the finished product's tone and content.

Two of the earliest examples of this type of collaboration are Showtime's movie *In the Company of Spies* (1999) and the CBS television series *The Agency* (2001–2003). Directed by Tim Matheson and written by Roger Towne, *In the Company of Spies* was a Paramount Studios production featuring Karl Pruner as a CIA operative who is captured and eventually executed by North Korean officials. In order to retrieve the officer and the information he uncovered before his death, Pruner's superiors bring an operative out of retirement (Tom Berenger) to lead a small team dedicated to the task. Based on a story written by the former CIA analyst Robert Cort, the film was originally envisioned as the first installment of a CIA-based film franchise.[1]

CBS's *The Agency* debuted two years after *In the Company of Spies* and was one of three spy shows that premiered just weeks after 9/11. But unlike its competitors, *Alias* and *24*, *The Agency* focused primarily on the inner workings of the CIA rather than on dramatic action and suspense. The show's central cast featured the director of the CIA, a few special operations officers, and a small band of employees from the Directorate of Science and Technology. Gil Bellows, Gloria Reuben, Paige Turco, Beau

Bridges, and Ronny Cox played the starring roles. Michael Frost Beckner, the screenwriter for *Spy Game* (2001), created and wrote for the series.

Both *In the Company of Spies* and *The Agency* received substantial support from the CIA, since it hoped these texts would reassure Americans about the continued need for Langley in the post–Cold War era, boost employee morale, encourage recruitment, and put a human face on the Agency. This was especially important to the CIA since both texts were created *before* the events of 9/11, when the CIA was suffering from attrition, congressional attacks, and a lack of strong public support (see chapter 2). Given that *The Agency* debuted just weeks after 9/11, however, this show actually helped deflect criticisms launched at the CIA for failing to foresee the attacks, and, according to the series creator, led the outfit to use the show as both a tool of psychological warfare and a threat-scenario workshop during the war on terror's early stages. Thus *In the Company of Spies* and *The Agency* served markedly different functions from the CIA's perspective.

CIA Cooperation: The Means and the Ends

The CIA assisted *In the Company of Spies* in numerous ways. For instance, Roger Towne visited the Langley campus and worked with the PAO for over a year developing and revising his script.[2] According to Bill Harlow, Towne also worked one-on-one with Chase Brandon, "bouncing ideas off him and sending scripts in" for feedback.[3] Brandon also visited the producers on set, where he again offered suggestions on final additions to the script,[4] and the film's actors spent several days at CIA headquarters preparing for their roles as Agency officers. Tom Berenger met with Director George Tenet and the associate deputy director of operations, and toured the Operations Center and the Balkan Task Force. Ron Silver, who played the director of central intelligence, also met with Tenet and his deputy director in a separate visit,[5] while Alice Krige met with the director and the associate deputy director of intelligence, as well as Ombudsman Sharon Basso and several public affairs officers.[6] These meetings were intended to give the cast and crew a sense of the Agency's mission and its people, while the movie's producers and director also visited campus to get a "cinematographic flavor of the CIA Headquarters and its people."[7]

The CIA also allowed the crew of *In the Company of Spies* to shoot for more than twelve hours on location in its old headquarters lobby, first-floor corridors, and back gate in June 1998, something Langley rarely does. Nearly sixty Agency employees volunteered to be extras in the film to give the appearance of a typical day at work and to avoid the hassle of obtaining security clearances for outside actors trying to enter the campus. The Center for CIA Security also provided officers as extras, while three other officers served as stunt drivers doing high-speed driving through the back gate and in Washington, DC, traffic.[8]

In addition to Matheson's team, the CIA also welcomed Showtime, which sent a crew to film a behind-the-scenes look at the film, and *Entertainment Tonight*, which conducted interviews with Matheson, Berenger, CIA officials, and some of the extras for a promotional piece it ran on the film.[9] In October 1999, the CIA showcased the fruits of its labor by premiering *In the Company of Spies* at Langley. Among the five hundred CIA, Showtime, and Paramount guests were Federal Reserve Chairman Alan Greenspan, White House Chief of Staff John D. Podesta, ABC's Cokie Roberts, and NBC's Andrea Mitchell.[10]

CBS's *The Agency* received similar support. For instance, it became the first television program granted permission to film at CIA headquarters, and it used Agency employees as extras for the pilot. The show's department heads were also allowed to tour headquarters in order to recreate its offices, and they "bombarded" the PAO with "countless" inquiries.[11] Michael Frost Beckner also worked with Chase Brandon to develop the script for the pilot episode and submitted early drafts to Brandon, who approved of them enough to seek permission from his superiors to assist the series. "I think both Chase and Tenet agreed to assist us because, after reading my script," Beckner said, "they understood that *The Agency* was trying to take a really accurate look at the CIA without passing judgment. In other words, our show wasn't like *Alias* or those other extremely unrealistic programs that were in development at the time, and it also wasn't like a lot of films that featured CIA agents who eventually go rogue only to come back and try to assassinate the president."[12]

In exchange for receiving assistance with the pilot, *The Agency*'s executives agreed to premiere the program at Langley, but unlike *In the Company of Spies*, the television premiere never took place. "I still have the invitation framed on my wall, which asks me to 'RSVP no later than September 11, 2001,'" Beckner reflects. The premiere had been scheduled for September 21, 2001, but after the events of 9/11, the CIA could not officially continue its support of the series, as it had a much less immediate interest in devoting resources to a television program.[13]

As a result, *The Agency* relied on former CIA employees as technical consultants for the remainder of the series, including Tony and Jonna Mendez, long-serving veterans of the CIA's Directorate of Science and Technology, and Bazzel Baz, a former marine who also worked in CIA special operations. Their role was to provide advice to the series creators regarding setting, tradecraft, characters, plots, and understanding of official CIA procedures. Baz even went on to serve as the series associate producer in season 2, when Shaun Cassidy took over the program. As this chapter reveals below, however, Chase Brandon would still play an important role throughout the first season of *The Agency*, although that role took on a more informal, though perhaps more fascinating, nature.

The CIA's extensive support of these two projects was originally designed to help the filmmakers portray the Agency in a positive light, to reassure viewers of the need for intelligence during the post–Cold War era, and to retain and increase its applicant pool. As outlined in the previous chapter, the mid to late 1990s were dark times for the Agency: the collapse of the Soviet Union left the CIA devoid of a prominent enemy, and the Aldrich Ames case led to congressional hearings in which the dismantling of the Agency was discussed. These factors played an important role in the cuts to the Agency's budget and employment levels in the later half of the decade. In fact, George Tenet explains that by the mid to late 1990s, the intelligence budget was "in Chapter 11," having suffered a 10 percent cut over the course of the decade.[14] That budget never fully recovered until after 9/11, despite the fact that Tenet wrote personal letters to President Clinton in 1998 and 1999 asking for increases (which apparently succeeded only in "annoying the President").[15]

During the late 1990s, recruitment and employment levels had also decreased, as many employees left for more lucrative careers in the private sector, and internal morale was significantly low.[16] Tenet's director of public affairs, Bill Harlow, explained that the Agency was specifically suffering from the "peace dividend." After the fall of the Berlin Wall, he stated, "our workforce was cut by 25 percent, and this was done largely by attrition, so the Agency was prohibited from hiring very many people, which was disastrous. Tenet recognized the problem and worked hard to turn it around, but it took years to do so."[17] According to Harlow, things had begun to slowly improve by 1999, although the CIA was still "generally at war with the administration over its budget." Needless to say, "Recruitment was always in the back of our mind in public affairs. Whenever we could, we would do things which would help raise public awareness about the fact that we . . . had interesting and rewarding careers to offer to the right candidates, and that we had a lot of talented, dedicated, and honorable people on our staff."

In the Company of Spies

In the Company of Spies fell perfectly in line with this basic recruitment strategy. The film revolves around a team of specialists assembled to re-cover important intelligence that a captured CIA operative has gathered in North Korea. The team features a retired CIA operative as the leader, two Science and Technology employees, a field operative who is eventually de-ployed to North Korea, an intelligence analyst, a computer specialist, and a political psychologist. In other words, the employees are drawn from several of the CIA's directorates and give viewers a good introduction to the types of jobs each offers—something the CIA valued since most spy films feature only those working in the clandestine services.

Additionally, the film stresses the unique rewards of working for the Agency, a theme most explicitly explored through the character of Joanne Gertz (Elizabeth Arlen). Gertz is a satellite-image analyst who is planning to leave the CIA for the private sector, presumably because Kodak will pay her more money and because she has temporarily lost her "missionary zeal" for the Agency. Through working on the film's task force and helping to neutralize a nuclear threat, however, it is implied that Gertz rediscovers that zeal, coming to understand that the reward and sense of purpose that government work offers cannot be matched by the perks of the private sector. The same theme of a burned-out officer rediscovering the purpose and thrill of intelligence work is repeated in the characters of Kevin Jeffer-son and Dale Beckham. Beckham is a borderline alcoholic who is able to give up drinking only after witnessing his captured colleague, Marko (Pruner), being executed by the North Koreans, and thus sets out with renewed purpose and clarity to recover the intelligence Marko discovered. Likewise, Jefferson, who at the start of the film runs a successful Thai res-taurant, returns to the Agency to rediscover the thrill, pride, and purpose of intelligence, which is presumably unparalleled by the food industry.

The portrayals of these characters urged viewers to consider a career in government service while simultaneously encouraging current em-ployees to remain on staff despite employment reductions, budget cuts, and tempting offers from the private sector. They also encouraged former officers to consider returning to the Agency. Additionally, the CIA used its cooperation with *In the Company of Spies* to bolster internal morale through the PAO's newsletter, *What's News at CIA*. As one article explains, Ron Silver joined the cast after reading the script because in college he had "some crazy romance about the CIA and talked to an Agency recruiter since he had studied Chinese and later traveled in Russia."[18] "For me," he continued, "this script is a tribute to you people, who have decided to do something for us with your lives. . . . Thank you for making this life choice." Equal praise for CIA employees was featured in another article, where Brandon told colleagues that the cast and crew of *In the Company of Spies* were "impressed with the Agency and its officers."[19] The article then quoted Matheson's script assistant as saying that being at the CIA was "almost like a religious, spiritual experience," and that the actress Kim Roberts felt that "being inside the CIA [was] an unbelievable experience . . . and meeting real Agency officers is a true honor." Brandon's article then ended with a quote from Matheson, telling employees, "We are proud of the work we do to entertain the country's moviegoers, and by virtue of coming here and getting to know the Agency's people and its mission, we better understand the pride you feel in protecting America's freedoms. May God protect and bless the wonderful men and women of the Central Intelligence Agency." As these comments demonstrate, the CIA tried to use its cooperation with *In the Company of Spies* to boost the internal morale of the Agency, highlighting the idea that famed Hollywood players both admire and honor CIA officers (and find those individuals worthy of exploring in film). Bill Harlow believes that recruitment levels also increased after the film's release, although he admits that the CIA doesn't "have exact numbers on that."[20]

Outside of recruitment and morale purposes, *In the Company of Spies* also helped argue the CIA's case that it deserved an increase in budget. The film explicitly illustrates that threats to U.S. security have not dissipated simply because the Cold War ended, and thus that intelligence gathering is still vital. To hammer home this message, the mentally unstable leader of North Korea possesses nuclear technology and is now buying ICBMs from the Russians in order to acquire launch capabilities. The ICBMs would allow the North Koreans to deliver a nuclear attack capable of reaching the U.S. West Coast, not to mention the American and South Korean forces stationed in the DMZ. This intelligence is gathered only through Langley's efforts, and the scenario highlights the real CIA's concerns that many of Russia's arsenals were left unguarded during the collapse of the Soviet Union and were being traded to unpredictable regimes. The film also goes after the presidential administration for slashing the

CIA's budget, as Silver's DCI explicitly quips that the government expects the CIA to do the same amount of work that it has in the past, but then complains when it is unable to do so on a reduced budget and with less staff. The film also suggests that because of its slashed budget, the Agency has had to rely too much on technologically gathered intelligence rather than on human intelligence, and that its inability to recruit more spies has hurt the Agency's capacity to uncover vital information.

Finally, the film bolsters the CIA's public image by pitting the DCI against the national security adviser to present the Agency as a valorous, non-politicized institution. This is expressed most clearly in the film when the CIA's operative, Jack Marko, is captured in North Korea after discovering the country's plan to import Russian ICBMs to launch its nuclear arsenal. Instead of working to rescue Marko, the national security adviser simply wants to forget the trouble, calling Marko's capture a "political embarrassment" since the president is looking to strengthen the United States' relationship with the North Koreans. For the same reason, the adviser is also unwilling to accept information that Russia is supplying the Koreans with ICBMs, even though it's clear to viewers that this is the case. As one might expect from a CIA-Hollywood collaboration, the DCI refuses to let politics cloud his assessment of his team's intelligence gathering, and although surprised by the North Korean link to Russia, he encourages the president to act on his information and to blow up the ship carrying the ICBMs to port. The president ultimately ignores his national security adviser and follows the DCI's advice; when the CIA successfully curtails the nuclear threat, the president exclaims, "When the Agency is good, it's spectacular and no one even knows!"[21]

While the public reception of *In the Company of Spies* will be discussed below, this textual analysis demonstrates how the CIA's yearlong relationship with the film's writer and director resulted in a text that attempted to burnish the Agency's image, reassure viewers about the need for intelligence, encourage the public to support the CIA with greater resources, and potentially boost recruitment and internal morale at a low point in CIA history. Compared to Hollywood's history of depicting the CIA as rogue, immoral, or buffoonish, *In the Company of Spies* could be considered a great success in the eyes of the Agency. Given that the CIA invited prominent news journalists and the White House chief of staff to the film's premiere, it seems clear that the Agency was hoping to use the film to influence commentators' and powerful politicians' views on the Agency's performance and necessity.

In light of all these benefits, then, it is unsurprising that the CIA tried to duplicate this feat through its collaboration with *The Agency*. What neither the show's creators nor the CIA could have known, however, was just how timely this next project would prove to be, both in terms of the show's ripped-from-the-headlines plotlines and the CIA's need to deflect the sharp criticisms aimed at the organization in the immediate aftermath of 9/11.

The Agency

While *The Agency* began collaborating with Langley in early 2001, it aired just a few weeks after the 9/11 attacks and thus functioned much differently for the CIA than *In the Company of Spies*. By the time the show debuted on September 27, very few people questioned the *need* for an intelligence-gathering organization, and faced with a viable enemy once again, the CIA almost immediately enjoyed a resurgence in public support. In fact, the Knight Ridder News Service reported that Agency applications soared from an average of six hundred per week to nearly three thousand in the first week following 9/11.[22] *New York Magazine* also stated that from 2001 to 2002, the CIA experienced a 50 percent increase in applications overall.[23] Financial support for the Agency soon followed. In February 2002, John Lumpkin reported that the Bush administration had allocated an additional $1.5 to $2 billion for the CIA, bringing its annual budget to an estimated $5 billion.[24] This figure represented a nearly 45 percent increase over the previous year.

But while few Americans questioned the need for intelligence, the events of 9/11 led numerous sectors of society to question the *competence* of the community, especially as it related to the Agency's ability to detect, let alone foil, terrorist threats. For instance, late-night talk show hosts criticized the CIA and FBI for failing to share intelligence about the 9/11 hijackers and intensifications in the jihadist movement. The CIA knew that at least two of the hijackers were in the United States and posed a potential threat, but it failed to alert the FBI about their entry and whereabouts. In response to the failure, David Letterman quipped in 2001 that "the CIA announced that they now plan to cooperate more openly with the FBI. The just haven't told the FBI yet. . . . But if you think about it, the FBI and CIA are very competitive. In times of trouble, both agencies want to be the one to drop the ball."

Journalists and politicians also launched a series of criticisms at the Agency. Just one week after the attacks, Senator Richard Shelby, vice chairman and senior Republican of the Senate Intelligence Committee, argued that CIA Director George Tenet should resign given the Agency's failure to predict and prevent the assaults. In that same week, *The Independent*'s Phillip Knightley argued that the failure to prevent 9/11 was just one in a string of intelligence failures, and he even proclaimed that "American intelligence has never been very good, and since the end of the Cold War, it has grown fat and lazy."[25] Melvin Goodman made a similar argument in *Issues of Science and Technology*, but added that by abolishing its Office of Research and Development in 1998, the CIA was "no longer on the cutting edge of advanced technology in the fields of clandestine collection and satellite reconnaissance"; thus, he argued, the Agency would be "heavily dependent on the technology of outside contractors" during the war on terror.[26] This was particularly worrisome, Goodman concluded, since even the NSA had been caught off guard by "new fiber optic cables that cannot be tapped, encryption software that cannot be broken, and cell phone traffic that is too voluminous to be processed." Goodman therefore implied that the CIA had for years been in a poor position to fight global terrorism.

The prominent political commentator Fareed Zakaria also criticized the CIA in the *Washington Post* in February 2002. Zakaria admitted that while the CIA was the only organization in the U.S. government that took the threat from Osama bin Laden seriously before 9/11, the Agency still needed "fixing." He specifically complained that the Agency was a lumbering giant "structured to confront another hierarchical organization—such as the Soviet Union—not the shadowy, decentralized enemies of today." He also argued that the CIA was geared to share its information with the White House and the military, but that in the war on terror, it must now partner with the coast guard, the customs service, the Drug Enforcement Administration, and the FBI. Zakaria also claimed that the CIA had stopped taking important risks because, for the past twenty-five years, the White House "has hung the CIA out to dry every time it needed a scapegoat," and thus the Agency's first goal has long been "to stay out of trouble"—not to find "a path to intelligence success."

In this atmosphere, CBS's *The Agency* worked to deflect criticisms of the CIA by offering a reassuring image of the Agency's capabilities weekly. Consider, for instance, the show's pilot. In this episode, viewers learn that the CIA has identified al-Qaeda as a security threat and that members of the organization have for some time been planning a "major attack" in Europe. Luckily for Langley, one of their officers had been able to infiltrate al-Qaeda some time ago and provided the CIA with the attack date just before being caught and murdered by the terrorist group. The date leaves the CIA with only three days to discover and foil the plot, but through a combination of sharp analysis, high-tech software, and human intelligence, the Agency discovers that the cell is planning to bomb a large British department store. It then shares this information with British intelligence (which knows almost nothing of the plot) and helps to disrupt the attack at the last minute. The episode then ends with one of the characters saying that he hopes one day "all of our jobs will be obsolete." The message, of course, is that that day is not here yet. The pilot then ends with a close-up of an American flag waving outside while a character sits down at a piano to perform Todd Rundgren's elegiac "A Dream Goes on Forever."

Undoubtedly, the ending of this episode attempted to trade on Americans' heightened sense of patriotism in a melodramatic manner, but, nonetheless, the pilot depicted the Agency as one that had been trying to infiltrate al-Qaeda for years, shares intelligence when needed, and is able to garner the accurate human intelligence necessary to prevent terrorist attacks. Of course, the timing of the episode was eerie, as it was set to debut just two weeks after 9/11, and it was eventually rescheduled for early November 2001 when the emotional sting of the al-Qaeda attacks had begun to soften. Nonetheless, the episode was just one of several in the series that depicted the CIA regularly defeating terrorism, even when the threats came from outside the box.

To cite just one example, "The Plague Year" features an Algerian terrorist who has altered his skin, eyes, and hair in order to appear white so that he may evade detection within the United States. The episode starts with the CIA monitoring and translating a conversation between the Algerian and his handler, as the pair approaches the U.S. border from Mexico. The conversation indicates that the man is a suicide bomber, and thus the CIA begins to monitor him with a combination of thermal imagery, video surveillance, and a recorder hidden in the handler's ring in order to find out who will deliver the bomb to him. It turns out, however, that the Algerian is not planning a suicide bombing; rather, he has been infected with smallpox and is hoping to get arrested during the most contagious stage of his disease so that he can infect as many law enforcement officials as possible. The CIA is able to discover the plot through its analysis of signals collection and investigative research in time to vaccinate those who came in contact with the terrorist, despite the fact that recent events had conditioned officers to focus on Arab terrorists toting bomber vests. The episode also features the CIA working with the Department of Homeland Security in order to accomplish this goal, and thus suggests that the CIA is ready for just about anything and can effectively play well with others.

Unsurprisingly, these types of episodes pleased the CIA immensely. Chase Brandon even argued in 2001 that "right now the American public needs a sense of reassurance," and thus a show like *The Agency* "couldn't be more timely."[27] But the show—whose very tagline was "Now, more than ever, we need the CIA"—did not just help reassure viewers about Langley's capabilities and necessity; some episodes also worked to construct the moral supremacy of the CIA, and therefore put their plotlines in conversation with current events in a way that helped the Agency further deflect criticism. A case in point is "Rules of the Game," aired on December 6, 2001. Just four weeks earlier, the CIA and FBI had both come under attack for their push to sanction torture in the war on terror. Alexander Cockburn of *The Nation*, for example, reminded readers that torture is deemed illegal both under the Eighth Amendment, which prevents cruel and unusual punishment, and international covenants signed and ratified by the United States. The United States would do well, Cockburn noted, to rethink its recent use of torture on detainees, especially since the CIA's past use of torture garnered little viable information.[28] The outspoken civil libertarian Alan Dershowitz also weighed in on the subject. He told the *60 Minutes* correspondent Mike Wallace that in cases of a "ticking bomb," where fast information would save lives, investigators should be able to go to a judge and obtain a torture warrant. But he warned that there should be oversight of all torture situations, because "if anybody has any doubt that our CIA, over time, has taught people to torture, has encouraged torture, has probably itself tortured in extreme cases, I have a bridge to sell you in Brooklyn."[29] These comments, and others like them, depicted the CIA as a torture-happy organization whose behavior is illegal, unregulated, and morally suspect at best. The same image of the Agency had, of course, been circulating in Hollywood for decades.

But this was not the image of the CIA presented in *The Agency*. In "Rules of the Game," the Israelis trick the CIA into handing over a terrorist for interrogation, claiming that the man the CIA captured in a recent raid was really an Israeli spy that had infiltrated the cell. The Israelis employ mild torture methods to interrogate the prisoner, but their efforts fail to yield results. When the Mossad asks the CIA if they want the terrorist transferred to an Israeli military prison or to the Saudis, who use more "persuasive" means of getting people to talk, the Agency requests that the terrorist remain in a military prison. The Mossad chief then asks when Americans will learn to do what is necessary to defeat terrorism. If the terrorist were to go to the United States, the chief points out, he would be subject to an American jury, lawyers, and the legal system, all the while "being allowed to remain silent." The Israeli suggests that the Saudis are a better option because they can torture him until he speaks, but the Americans find the idea morally reprehensible; in they end, they get the information they need, not through torture, but through a combination of technological and human intelligence.

These portrayals of the CIA as a competent, well-equipped, and morally upright Agency stemmed, in part, from the CIA's assistance during the pilot, which set the patriotic, pro-Agency tone for the entire series. The use of the Mendezes and Baz as technical consultants also had an effect. In my interview with Baz, for instance, it was clear that he was invested in protecting the image of the Agency. He specifically stated that in government circles, the CIA is often known as the "bastard stepchild of the government bureaucracy. But it is filled with real Americans, real patriots, whose primary job is to collect intelligence."[30] Since the CIA is sometimes disparaged by its own government, both he and the CIA were interested in working "with the show to help give [the Agency] a good name," he stated. He continued by claiming that he got "certain calls from people at the CIA" who said they were glad that he was working on the show—"that they had an honest face on the inside, someone . . . that would encourage the producers not to abuse the good nature of so many hardworking patriots at the CIA who have given their lives in service for their country."

The Agency: Beyond the Pilot

While the assistance of Baz and the Mendezes helped set the tone for the series, the public record suggests that the CIA and Chase Brandon were not involved with the series after the pilot, but this is not the case. In our phone conversations, Beckner explained that through his initial contacts with Brandon, the two developed a "strong friendship."[31] This resulted in Beckner occasionally calling Brandon to check on the feasibility of something he was writing about, and Brandon calling Beckner to offer up ideas about the show's story lines. "Because these conversations were so casual," noted Beckner, "I'm not sure that I would classify them as official CIA-Hollywood exchanges; you know, sometimes it's just so hard to tell with the CIA what counts as official because they have a way of communicating what they want without making you feel like it is a 'government message,' per se."

Nonetheless, these conversations led to the development of several season 1 story lines, and Beckner suggests that Brandon and the CIA may have envisioned *The Agency* as a useful intimidation tool and a threat-scenario workshop in addition to its function as a way to help the CIA burnish its image in a tumultuous time. For instance, the pilot, Beckner explains:

> was based on the premise that Bin Laden attacks the West and a war on terrorism invigorates the CIA.[32] When this took place two weeks before the pilot aired, we pulled the broadcast of that episode and saved it for later in the season. Three more times in season 1, I wrote/produced episodes that predicted events in the war on terrorism. One episode involved a Predator drone outfitted with a Hellfire missile that allows the CIA to remotely attack a Pakistani general. Another involved an anthrax attack on Americans, while yet another revolved around a Russian suitcase bomb that had been stolen from the former USSR. All of these events came to pass shortly before or after these episodes aired (and in fact, the anthrax episode had to be pulled when the story about the lethal mailings occurred the day our episode was supposed to air).

Beckner claimed that his unofficial conversations with Chase had a lot to do with the CIA show's ability to "predict" these specific events, since they were all plotlines Chase had pitched to him in their conversations. In other words, the plots for all four episodes originated from the CIA, although it was Beckner who fleshed them out into script form.

Beckner claims that he is not sure why Chase called him to suggest these ideas, and the CIA director of public affairs at the time, Bill Harlow, argues there was "no magic" involved in the show's ability to predict the headlines.[33] The CIA had been worried about al-Qaeda for years, Harlow stated: "Director Tenet in Congress was saying in 1999–2000 that they could strike at any time." The Agency was also very worried about anthrax and biological warfare, he continued, and again this can be found in public testimony: "As to the Hellfire missiles, these were a big issue for us post-9/11 as we were rapidly trying to get that capability. I mean we were getting surveillance videos that saw Bin Laden in Afghanistan, and we wished we had the capability to take him out. . . . All of these conversations were percolating around the Agency, including the Public Affairs

Office." Harlow then went on to argue that the ability to inform writers about contemporary issues is one advantage an entertainment liaison provides the entertainment industry, and *The Agency* simply got lucky that the headlines intersected with its storylines so neatly.

Beckner, however, remains unconvinced. His sense is that Chase Brandon was "attempting to test the waters somehow,"[34] and when further pressed, he suggested that the CIA may have been using the series to workshop threat scenarios, as they were already doing with the University of Southern California's Institute for Creative Technologies (ICT).[35] The idea is not as crazy as it sounds. Shortly after 9/11, President Bush sent his senior adviser, Karl Rove, to Los Angeles to meet with entertainment leaders to discuss ways they could "encourage volunteerism and offer support for American troops."[36] Screenwriters and directors such as David Fincher and Spike Jonze also "brainstormed with Pentagon officials about creative ways to prevent future terrorist attacks,"[37] all as part of a larger Hollywood-military effort.

The ICT often organizes such efforts to unite government officials and Hollywood creators. According to Richard Lindhelm, the institute's peacetime purpose is to set the "best minds of the entertainment industry to the task of creating state-of-the-art training exercises for soldiers," and more recently, to create possible terrorist scenarios for government consideration.[38] "Fortunately or unfortunately," Lindhelm argued, "art has often led the way to reality, and art and writers and motion pictures and ideas coming from writers have often been the inspiration for reality."[39] (Tom Clancy's 1994 novel *Debt of Honor* is often cited in such discussions, as it featured a disgruntled Japanese pilot intentionally flying an airplane into the U.S. Capitol Building, thereby killing most of the top government officials.) In 2002, the CIA formally recognized the link between entertainment and reality, too, as it began working with the ICT on a video game that would allow Agency analysts to assume the role of terror-cell leaders, members, and operatives in order to help the United States avert future attacks.[40]

Beckner claims that he was asked to join the ICT think tank while working on *The Agency*. At the time of the invitation, he stated, he was helping Shannon Spann work with the producers who had purchased the rights to her husband's story (Shannon is the widow of Johnny "Mike" Spann, the CIA's first casuality in Afghanistan, and she, herself, served as a CIA officer). Through that project, Beckner and Spann had become friends, and one day a CIA officer in Los Angeles asked the writer to lunch to thank him for helping Spann navigate the film industry. That contact (whom Beckner would not name) then mentioned that the CIA works with the USC think tank to workshop threat scenarios, and Michael was then invited to participate. When Beckner followed up with Chase Brandon regarding the opportunity, however, Brandon told him that he "really shouldn't waste [his] time with that": "He told me that what you're doing with *The Agency* certainly makes us happy enough."

This comment certainly is cryptic, and Beckner did not elaborate. Nonetheless, it suggests that in Brandon's eyes, Beckner's work on *The Agency* served the same purpose as the ICT think tank, which uses screenwriters to think through terrorist attacks and other threats to national security. By suggesting particular plotlines, then, Brandon may have been feeding Beckner ideas that the CIA wanted to see developed, explored, and analyzed precisely because it knew they were serious threats. And admittedly, Beckner is very good at this type of writing.

The creator of *Spy Game*, Beckner excels at crafting stories that are politically, psychologically, and technologically intricate, and *The Agency* certainly gave intelligence analysts new scenarios to ponder. The episode dealing with a terrorist self-infected with small pox is one example, especially as the terrorist and his handler worked to purposely get caught in order to infect senior government officials. But other episodes were similarly inventive. "A Slight Case of Anthrax," for instance, featured a European named Zimmer planning a biological attack on Americans. In the episode, Zimmer acquires the same anthrax the American government developed and sold to Iraq when Iraq was its ally in the fight against Iran. But the Iraqis had taken the American sample and made a strain resistant to antibiotics, and that strain now poses a danger to the United States. The episode shows the CIA defeating the threat, but it also asks analysts to consider how foreign terrorists might acquire anthrax and how the U.S. government might prevent a resistant strain from spreading.

A similar element appeared in "The Peacemakers," which features a growing military buildup on the border of India (in response to Pakistani terrorist attacks in Indian territory). The episode involves the CIA and the Department of Homeland Security trying to figure out how to avoid a World War III, especially when a rogue Pakistani general decides to initiate an attack against India's forces without higher military permission. The United States wants to assassinate the rogue general, but it cannot kill him inside Pakistan without provoking a fundamentalist coup. The problem is compounded by the fact that the Pakistani military will not admit that it cannot control its own general. As a result, the CIA decides to kill the general using a Predator drone outfitted with a Hellfire missile, and it then presents a fake photograph to both India and Pakistan "confirming" that the general was killed by an unprovoked attack from terrorist forces. While both sides realize the story is a lie, they agree to it in order to prevent further tensions. The story's resolution is creative and addressed a serious anxiety about Indian and Pakistani relations. It also envisioned the Predator drone attack, which the CIA had not been able to execute at that point. According to Beckner, Brandon especially encouraged him to develop that element of the storyline to "see how the whole thing might play out."

On at least one other occasion, Brandon also pushed an inaccurate storyline concerning the CIA's technological capabilities. According to Beckner, while he often consulted with Chase to enhance the realism of the show's surveillance and computer-based technology, Brandon once suggested featuring a highly advanced biometric system that would allow officials to detect almost any terrorist entering the United States. Beckner remarked that at first, he was unsure why Brandon was pushing the plotline in their conversations given that the device was so futuristic. "It would've been such a great tool in the war on terrorism if we had actually had it," he remarked. Brandon conceded that the technology was not real, but "he told me to go ahead and put it in the episode anyway," because "it would scare them." The "them," of course, meant plotting terrorists, since, according to Chase, "terrorists watch TV, too."[41]

This exchange between Beckner and Brandon suggests that Chase was using *The Agency* to scare potential and existing terrorists by exaggerating the CIA's ability to track their activities and ultimately to capture them. (The same motive may have also been at play in "The Peacemakers," as terrorists may have well feared that any Predator drone in their area was outfitted with a bomb.) Admittedly, the strategy was a smart one, as Brandon is right that many terrorists consume American media. Simultaneously, however, the strategy belies the CIA's claim that it is invested in Hollywood only to portray accurately the Agency and to educate viewers about the CIA's role. Indeed, these examples suggest that the CIA had started to use the American media much as it did in the Cold War—not just as a tool of self-aggrandizement, but also as part of a psychological warfare strategy.

Beckner's comments also demonstrate that the CIA's involvement in Hollywood is indeed shadowy and difficult to trace, especially since its interactions often take place only between two well-placed individuals, either in person or over the phone. After all, Beckner stated that almost everything he did with the CIA was done on a handshake and a phone call;

in the public domain, the timeliness of *The Agency*'s episodes were chalked up to the nature of the drama, or the use of ex-CIA technical consultants. As *The Agency*'s publicist, Tracey Rabb, argued, "You really can't do a serious drama about the CIA without colliding with topical events"[42]; and CNN's Lauren Hunter explained how the show's creators actually read intelligence manuals and conferred with ex-CIA officers to achieve the show's realism.[43] Neither account suggested that the CIA or its entertainment liaison was still active in shaping the content of the series, and without Beckner's revelations, this fact would remain hidden.

Critical Reception and Conclusions

In total, *The Agency* and *In the Company of Spies* were intended to provide a boon to the CIA in the pre-9/11, post–Cold War era. *In the Company of Spies* showcased the Agency's employees in a positive light when recruitment levels were down, argued for a greater budget at a time when the Agency's finances were being cut, and highlighted new threats when many Americans questioned the need for the CIA's continued existence. The CIA even invited several influential reporters and politicians to the film's premiere, in what appears to have been an attempt to subject them to pro-CIA propaganda masquerading as a fun evening out. And even the film's creators toed the line by singing the CIA's praises in press materials. The *New York Times*, for instance, quoted Matheson as praising Agency employees for their "tremendous passion" and for answering "to a higher calling." "By and large," he continued, "the people I met at the agency are very dedicated, extremely intelligent and have extremely broad knowledge of the politics of the world and our place in it."[44] The producers of CBS's *The Agency* intended it to give the CIA similar treatment, as it, too, depicted Langley in a positive light; in fact, the show was scheduled to premiere at a red-carpet event on campus on September 21, 2001. The events of 9/11 prevented that debut, but the show's timing did help the CIA conduct damage control at a time when critics were already blaming the Agency for a massive intelligence failure, calling for the director's resignation, and demanding a complete restructuring of the organization.

Precisely because of the CIA's heavy involvement in these projects, however, *The Agency* and *In the Company of Spies* were not without their critics, highlighting the fact that even loose government propaganda efforts do not always generate the desired effect. For instance, *Entertainment Weekly* gave *In the Company of Spies* a C-, calling it an "unabashed pro-spook PSA" that revolves around "pedestrian plotting . . . and an unrelenting portrayal of all Asians as dull-witted and bloodthirsty."[45] Matthew Campbell of the *Sunday Times* likewise took a jab at the CIA and the film, quipping that if the writers are so concerned with realism, "the CIA can only hope" that this will not "mean a scene in which agents rely on outdated maps, a mistake that resulted in America's destruction of the Chinese embassy in Belgrade [in 1999]."[46]

Some reviews of *The Agency* also reflected misgivings about Hollywood-CIA collaborations. David Grove, for instance, suggested that the CIA's involvement in the series constituted little more than propaganda, noting that in the series, "the CIA is righteous," and that the "first few episodes appeal to our newly heightened patriotic sensibilities."[47] What are we to think, Grove asks, when a burned-out official facing budget cuts exclaims, "People think the world has changed. Some even believe that this is an antiquated organization. But you and I know better"? Grove goes on to assert that while the series attempts to ask how far governmental agencies should go to fight evil, it is still unwilling to explore the CIA's more unsavory activities: "Instead, *The Agency* substitutes hardware for nuance . . . and omits moral complexities inside the CIA itself. Everything bad takes place outside the building."

The FAIR.org contributor Jeff Cohen seconded Grove in his article *"The Agency* on CBS: Right Time but Wrong Show." Here, Cohen posits that the American public needed an independent look at the Agency in the aftermath of 9/11, rather than the reassuring one that the CIA-Hollywood collaboration offered viewers. "In light of Sept. 11," he wrote, "Americans have a right to question how [the CIA] has performed lately and what sort of people it has been associating with, in Afghanistan and in other secret wars. These questions could be posed in a dramatic series but not on a show inclined more toward glorification than elucidation." Therefore, as long as CBS and the CIA remain wedded, viewers could not expect "hardhitting episodes" on the CIA's past alliance with terrorist organizations or the Agency's role in the bombings of a pharmaceutical factory in Sudan and the Chinese embassy in Serbia.

One of *The Agency*'s most scathing reviews came from Lewis Lapham, who wrote in *Harper's Magazine* that the series functioned as unwarranted propaganda for an intelligence community prone to arrogance, deceit, and outright stupidity.[48] His article went on to detail the ways the Agency has bungled numerous international conflicts over the last fifty years, noting that CBS could have hardly taken on a more ambitious project than attempting to legitimize an agency well-known for "chronic

stupidity and criminal incompetence." For Lapham, *The Agency* was part
of the CIA's attempts to promote a revival of the "atmospherics of the
Cold War," where the United States was once again "threatened by rogue
states, starving mobs, Arab terrorists, deadly chemicals, and treacherous
Chinese."

These reactions help explain why producers and the CIA may be invested in hiding their relationship, since known government influence on
a text often leads to cries of ill-intentioned propaganda. Each of these
comments also reveals the complexity of media texts and audiences, and
support Stuart Hall's idea that viewers do not always adopt the encoded
or dominant message of any given text. Rather, viewers also negotiate and
oppose a text's encoded message, or approach different segments from
multiple positions.[49] Indeed, *The Agency* was the shortest-lived and least
popular of the three spy shows that debuted in the fall of 2001 (*Alias* and
24 were the others), and interestingly, it was also the most celebratory,
suggesting that Americans were not fully ready to embrace the do-good
image of the CIA so soon after 9/11. Of course, these criticisms and complexities would not prevent the CIA from continuing its work with the
Hollywood community. Only encouraged by the perceived success of *In
the Company of Spies* and *The Agency*, the Public Affairs Office and its entertainment liaisons would continue to work with film and television producers on a variety of projects in order to boost recruitment, deflect criticisms, establish important industry contacts, and more. These projects
involved a range of investment levels on the CIA's part, but each helped
the Agency to revamp its image in the post–Cold War and post-9/11 eras,
as the next chapter demonstrates.

CHAPTER 4

The Chase Brandon Years

In the Company of Spies (1999) and *The Agency* (2001–2003) were two of the earliest projects to receive CIA assistance, but they were certainly not the only ones. In fact, Chase Brandon's term as entertainment industry liaison officer was prolific. From 1996 to 2007, he assisted numerous projects, including *Enemy of the State* (1998), *Alias* (2001–2006), *24* (2001–2010), *Bad Company* (2002), *The Sum of All Fears* (2002), *The Bourne Identity* (DVD, 2003), *The Recruit* (2003), *Fard Ayn* (in preproduction), and *The Rogue* (in preproduction). By associating themselves with the CIA, these filmmakers were able to market their work as "authentic," "accurate," and a "rare insider's look" at the Agency, but what exactly did the CIA seek to gain from their collaborations, and what has been the impact of these films more broadly?

The answer is multifaceted. First, the CIA attempted to use these projects for recruitment purposes. Second, some of these films helped Langley to reinvent itself after the Cold War and deflect specific post-9/11 criticisms aimed at the Agency. These films also allowed the CIA to project itself as an omnipresent and omnipotent entity—an image that has served it well for decades. The CIA's broader relationship with those in the motion picture industry has also helped the Agency boost internal morale, encourage future cinematic relationships, and even benefit in the field of covert action.

Of course, a single film rarely accomplishes all these objectives, but these categories are indicative of the wide range of benefits the CIA enjoys from its collaborative efforts. While a few of these same benefits were explored in the previous chapter, a discussion of *The Agency* and *In the Company of Spies* alone does not indicate the breadth and nature of the CIA's influence in Hollywood. As a result, this chapter explores several

CIA-assisted texts and the benefits they reaped, beginning with *Alias* and *The Recruit*.

Mission: Recruitment

The CIA always hopes that its work with the motion picture industry will boost recruitment and interest in the Agency. When headquarters backed *The Classified Files of the CIA* in the mid-1990s, for instance, it was hoping the show would serve as its own *Top Gun*—a film that generated great interest in the navy's air program and sent application numbers through the roof. Additionally, Chase Brandon praised *The Agency*'s recruitment value by relating that when he was approached by the CIA in the 1970s, "it was 'Hey, kid, come work for us even though we can't tell you what you are going to be doing.'"[1] When the CBS series was on, however, Brandon argued that the CIA could simply tell potential recruits, "If you want to know what we do, watch *The Agency* on Thursday nights." Even the CIA attorney John Rizzo recognized the importance of Hollywood for recruitment. In 2007, he argued that *In the Line of Fire* (1993) functioned as a "hell of a recruitment tool" for the Secret Service and articulated his hopes that Langley would soon find its cinematic equivalent.[2]

"Garnering" Recruits with *Alias*

The CIA's efforts to improve its Hollywood image indirectly work to bolster applications, but the Agency also liaises directly with the film community toward this same end. Most famously, the CIA collaborated with Jennifer Garner in 2004 to produce a recruitment video on its behalf. At the time, Garner was the star of the ABC "spy-fi" series *Alias*, which Chase Brandon worked on during season 1 as a technical consultant. The video features a medium shot of the then-thirty-one-year-old actress calling on citizens to join the intelligence service. In her segment, Garner states:

> I'm Jennifer Garner. I play a CIA officer on the ABC TV series *Alias*. In the real world, the CIA serves as our country's first line of defense in the ongoing war against international terrorism. CIA's mission is clear and direct: safeguard America and its people. And it takes smart people with wide-ranging talents and diverse backgrounds to carry out this mission—

people with integrity, common sense, patriotism, and courage. The kind of people who have always worked for the Agency.

But since the tragic events of 9/11, the CIA has an even stronger need for creative, innovative, flexible men and women from diverse backgrounds and a broad range of perspectives. Right now, the CIA has important, exciting jobs for U.S. citizens, especially those with foreign-language skills. Today, the collection of foreign intelligence has never been more vital for national security. If you're an American citizen and seek a challenging, rewarding career where you can make a difference in the world and here at home, contact the agency at www.cia.gov. Thank you.[3]

In heavily circulated press releases, the CIA claimed that Garner was selected to appear in the advertisement because her character on the series "embodies the integrity, patriotism and intelligence the CIA looks for in its officers."[4] He also noted that "Miss Garner, both in character as agent Sydney Bristow and as herself, embodies the intelligence, enthusiasm and dedication that we're looking for. Our continuing efforts to enlist the best and the brightest" are "admirably served" by her support and participation, which adds a "human touch to the message we're trying to convey."[5] Another reason for her selection, however, was much more banal. According to Bill Harlow, Brandon's boss, Garner was chosen for the video because at the time *Alias* was more popular than the other CIA-assisted texts (with the exception of *24*), and Garner was a bigger star than anyone who appeared on shows like *The Agency*.[6] Indeed, shortly after the recruitment video's release, *Alias* was averaging 10.3 million viewers per episode, up from the 9.7 million who watched during its first season.[7] (The show was never considered a *major* hit for ABC, but it did have a large, dedicated, cult following.)

In many ways, the CIA's recruitment of Garner was a smart choice. Considered the brainchild of the creator and executive producer J. J. Abrams, *Alias* revolved around a female operative and her complicated work and family relationships. In the pilot, Sydney works for a black-ops division of the CIA named SD-6, which actually turns out to be a rogue terrorist organization simply posing as the CIA. The show's early seasons then deal with Sydney's attempts to destroy SD-6 by working as a double agent for the real CIA. Throughout the seasons, Bristow and her colleagues at Langley continually face new challenges as they battle terrorists and criminals; and while Sydney often faces hardships both within and outside the Agency, she nonetheless persists in her efforts to protect American national security.

Sydney's determined and resourceful nature was attractive to the CIA's public relations team, and the selection of a star with name recognition helped the video appeal to a wide range of viewers. But Garner helped the CIA in other ways, too. For instance, *Alias* often won its Sunday night time slot among the coveted eighteen- to forty-nine-year-old demographic and ranked second among teens during its first season.[8] This meant that Garner was an ideal candidate to help the CIA appeal to young professionals, those with graduate school experience, and soon-to-be college graduates, all of whom it targets in recruitment. In fact, Garner's video was not only posted on the CIA Careers website, but it was also screened at college job fairs throughout the country.

Second, the show depicted Bristow balancing her spy career with a personal life and graduate education, as early seasons feature the officer pursuing a master's degree in English and subplots revolve around her romantic relationships and social engagements. These elements of the show encouraged young professionals and college graduates to identify with Sydney, but they also disrupted popular notions that CIA recruits must "marry the Agency" in order to succeed. That Garner was one of just a handful of women to ever hold the leading role in a spy series also helped distance the CIA from its long-standing image as an old boys' network. Her face, in other words, helped to emphasize the changing nature of the intelligence workforce and the growing number of women who now work in each directorate. Additionally, *Alias* depicted espionage as a glamorous career requiring operatives to travel to exotic cities at a moment's notice, meet assets in swanky nightclubs, dress in haute couture, and sport James Bond–like gadgetry. Although this is certainly not an accurate image of the life of a CIA officer, it did endow the profession with an attractive glossiness that would have helped initial recruitment efforts for those familiar with the show.

What *is* surprising about the CIA's selection of Garner is that during its second and third seasons, when the advertisement debuted, *Alias* had begun presenting the CIA as a morally dubious agency that even engaged in torture and imprisonment without due process.[9] (The CIA assisted *Alias* only during its first season, to the best of my knowledge.) Episodes also constructed the CIA as monitoring Americans' private communications, which violates citizens' rights to privacy and the Agency's charter. It seems, however, that the real CIA was willing to risk viewers' intertextual association of Garner with the show's version of Langley. After all, only

Garner appears in the video, and she, more than anyone else on the series, serves as the show's moral compass. Or perhaps the show's moral ambiguity didn't really bother the CIA. As Sharon Sutherland and Sarah Swan point out, given the show's constant depictions of terrorism, the morally ambiguous means resorted to often seem necessary. Indeed, the creators ask viewers to accept that a war on terrorism cannot be fought on the usual terms of engagement. "Moral lines must soften and bend in order to accommodate the necessary weapons such a battle requires,"[10] Sutherland and Swan write—a message the real CIA would likely champion. In fact, at the same time as *Alias*'s debut, Cofer Black, director of the CIA's Counterterrorist Center, stated in a congressional hearing, "There was 'before' 9/11 and 'after' 9/11. After 9/11, the gloves come off."[11] Black turned out to be referring to the CIA's global program of extraordinary rendition, which it used to kidnap and often torture detainees "in a system of secret prisons, some run by the CIA and some by foreign governments."[12] But the "gloves come off" mentality jived well with the later seasons of *Alias* (and *24*), which often featured its protagonists performing morally duplicitous acts in the name of national security—and often succeeding because of them.

The Recruit DVD

Sometimes the CIA's use of Hollywood to achieve its recruitment objectives is not as obvious as Garner's appearance in a promotional video. Occasionally, the Agency's promotions (outside a feature film) are more subtle, often masquerading as an informational feature on a DVD. Such is the case on *The Recruit* DVD (2003), which includes a sixteen-minute special titled "Spy School: Inside the CIA Training Program." This segment features Chase Brandon telling viewers about the recruitment, training, and career of a CIA officer. The entertainment liaison specifically explains that while the CIA receives thousands of applications each year, 99 percent of them are rejected because the applicants do not have the skill set the Agency needs. On the select 1 percent who interests them, Langley will run IQ tests, personality assessments, and background checks before deciding whether to invite applicants to "The Farm"—the main CIA training facility. At The Farm, recruits learn parachuting, demolitions, agent acquisition, surveillance, disguise, secret writing, photography, and more. Brandon also explains that graduating from The Farm entitles one to a job at the CIA, but that there are drawbacks to a life as a case officer.

Namely, these men and women work long hours, constantly travel, often stand in harm's way, and regularly deal with unsavory people.

On paper, this description sounds like a balanced and informational look at the CIA's recruitment and training process, but Brandon's comments are often intercut with scenes from the film in a way that points to the feature's dual recruitment purpose. These scenes feature the film's CIA recruiter, Walter Burke (Al Pacino), talking about how difficult it is to graduate from The Farm (many drop out or are asked to leave), and how challenging the spy profession can be. This editing strategy encourages viewers to question whether they have what it takes to work at the Agency (or at least to envision CIA officers as an elite, highly gifted group of people). The film's sense of recruitment is also heightened by Brandon's use of the second person in some of his descriptions. For instance, he states that training on The Farm is "one of the biggest adventures you'll ever have because you will live and work and train with people who will be your friends and your colleagues and your brethren for the rest of your life." His use of the second person directly invites viewers to envision themselves as CIA recruits, and Brandon's use of the verb "will" suggests that viewers indeed have what it takes to graduate from The Farm. The segment also ends on a melodramatic recruitment note, as Brandon argues that despite some career drawbacks, the "grandeur, the glory, the sense of purpose, the sense of accomplishment . . . the incredible sense of privilege and pride" involved in working for the CIA "so outweighs anything else" that people are still eager to serve the Agency.

These communication techniques are subtle, and less media-savvy viewers may be inclined to interpret the piece as more informational than manipulative—a reading amplified by the fact that Chase Brandon is never identified in the segment as an entertainment liaison or even as a Public Affairs Officer. Rather, Brandon is introduced only as a twenty-five-year veteran of the CIA who has worked in "various positions" but spent most of his career in covert operations. This description is accurate, but it hides the fact that at the time the video was produced, the CIA paid Brandon to paint a positive image of the Agency and to drum up support for the outfit. This omission de-emphasized the already-subtle recruitment slant of the film by leading viewers to interpret his picture of the CIA as one presented from an independent perspective.

This omission again reveals that CIA propaganda is often hard to detect by the average viewer; however, the failure to properly identify Brandon was the fault of the feature's producer, and thus demonstrates how Hollywood creators are also interested in promoting the CIA, whether it be for professional, political, or commercial reasons. Indeed on "Spy School," *The Recruit*'s producer, Jeff Apple, glorifies the Agency when he tells viewers that working for the CIA is the most thankless job in all of law enforcement and one of the most complicated. The public does not realize "the risks these people take to gather the intelligence to help our government figure out what do we have to do" to assess and defeat security threats. Apple declares, "I can tell you right now that there have been many averted terrorist acts that we'll never know about" because the CIA was successful at stopping them. He also tells viewers that we now live in a world of complication, and "that's why human intelligence is that much more important." Apple's comments encourage viewers to see CIA officers as selfless patriots and hint at the idea that the Agency should be given more funding to develop human intelligence abroad. It is not clear what motivated the producer's comments, but they do reveal that sympathetic creators are often as invested in supporting the CIA as the Agency itself.

Improving the Agency's Image

In fact, sympathetic writers, directors, and producers have always been instrumental to the CIA's public relations campaign, especially in the months and years that followed September 11, 2001. During this period, the CIA suffered a number of criticisms in the news media and on Capitol Hill, many of which found their way into *The 9/11 Report*. This report generally depicted American intelligence organizations as outdated because they were designed to fight just a handful of nation-states during the Cold War, not the global, cellular fronts of the war on terror. In terms of the CIA specifically, *The 9/11 Report* added that the Agency's analytic and human intelligence capabilities were too weak, and that it needed a stronger language program and a renewed emphasis on recruiting diversity among operations officers. The report also argued that the CIA needed to better manage human source and signals collections, and that Langley needed to better coordinate with other government agencies.[13]

The report also argued that the director of central intelligence had been stretched too thin, as he attempted to run the CIA, manage the loose confederation of U.S. intelligence agencies, and serve as the analyst in chief to the executive branch—something no recent DCI has done effectively.[14] This argument would eventually lead to the rearrangement of the U.S. intelligence community in 2004, which stripped the DCI of its role as the coordinator of all fifteen intelligence branches and replaced the post with the newly created Director of National Intelligence. This shift significantly diminished the power and influence of the DCI within the U.S. government by confining the office's domain to the CIA alone.

An outdated, overstretched, and ineffectual CIA, however, was not the image reflected in several popular films that debuted in the aftermath of 9/11. Indeed, this was the time when the CIA's efforts in improving its image through motion pictures had finally started to pay off, a fact partially demonstrated by the release of *The Recruit* and *The Sum of All Fears*. A textual analysis of these films reveals how the CIA worked with filmmakers to reinvent its image in the post-9/11 era, and how that image strongly contradicted that of an outdated Agency weak on human intelligence, analysis, and language capabilities.

The Recruit Revisited

As mentioned above, *The Recruit* stars Al Pacino as Walter Burke, a veteran recruiter and trainer for the CIA.[15] The film was released in 2003 and grossed roughly $52 million during its domestic run and a little over $100 million worldwide, making it a modest commercial success.

At the start of the film, Burke convinces James Clayton (Colin Farrell), an unconventional but brilliant MIT student, to join the Agency. Clayton then undergoes CIA assessment testing and a rigorous training program at The Farm, where he develops both his tradecraft and his romantic feelings for Layla Moore (Bridget Moynahan). While the film plays on the mutual attraction between Moore and Clayton, the main plotline focuses on the way that Burke is using his two recruits to unknowingly steal a software program from inside the CIA, so that he can sell it on the black market and then set up Moore and Clayton for the fall.

By several accounts, Chase Brandon was very involved in the development of *The Recruit*. He and the film's screenwriter, Roger Towne, had already worked together on *In the Company of Spies*, and according to the film's producers, Brandon was "instrumental in giving his insight into the Agency's facilities, methods, and complex recruitment process," including the ways the Agency "identifies suitable candidates, recruits them, and molds them into operation officers."[16] Bill Harlow concurred that Brandon exerted a significant influence on the story's development, suggesting ideas in preproduction and production that eventually made their way into the final cut.[17] While Harlow declined to give too many specifics, he did point to the scene in which Burke performs a magic trick by ripping up a newspaper and then making it appear whole during his recruitment pitch to Clayton. According to Harlow, DCI John McLaughlin often performed this trick, and Chase suggested it to the creators, arguing that it was a good way to show what interesting characters past CIA officers have been.

In addition to pitching story ideas and shaping the filmmakers' understanding of the Agency, Brandon also arranged for the producers, directors, and crew to visit CIA headquarters so they could see "how the operation works and what the people are like,"[18] and he served as an on-set adviser in Toronto. Reportedly, Chase was even cast to play a small role in the film but suffered a back injury just before shooting and thus was unable to appear.[19] The Agency's cooperation on the film, however, was not exhaustive. Harlow states that earlier versions of *The Recruit* showed the CIA in a much more positive light, but that subsequent revisions devolved from there. As a result, the CIA did not allow the crew to film on campus, although Brandon did assist them in recreating the headquarters lobby in Toronto, even measuring the distances between the stars on the memorial wall and the size of the statues so that they could be replicated on set with precision.[20]

The CIA's involvement with *The Recruit* allowed its creators to market the film as one "that for the first time opens the CIA's infamous closed doors and gives an insider's view into the Agency"[21] (even though *In the Company of Spies* had beat them to it). But Brandon's input during the film's development also helped the CIA counter some circulating criticisms about the Agency. For instance, at the start of *The Recruit*, Clayton tells Burke that he is uninterested in the CIA because "all he knows" is that "they are a bunch of old, fat, white guys who fell asleep at the wheel when we needed them most." An obvious reference to criticisms about the Agency failing to predict 9/11, Clayton's comment is quickly dismissed by Burke, who simply replies that the outsider doesn't "know shit." While the film never addresses in detail why Clayton's sentiment is inaccurate, Burke later stresses to his new recruits that the CIA's failures are known but its successes are not: "It's a company motto." Together, these scenes encouraged viewers to believe that the Agency did not twiddle its thumbs in the years leading up to the September 11 attacks, but, in fact, was busy identifying and averting numerous attacks just like it, albeit unbeknownst to the public. These elements of the film were almost certainly the result of Brandon's influence, as he frequently reinforced this same point in his public comments. To cite just one example, Brandon claimed in 2002 that the Agency has a covenant with the executive branch when it is told to execute a covert action: "If it's successful no one can know. The political credit is taken by the White House or Department of State. But when we fail . . . we alone take the blame so the president doesn't have to."[22] Brandon then reminded readers how President Kennedy once said that the "Agency's failures are always trumpeted and its successes never heralded." The same point was also parroted by Tom Berenger, one of the lead actors in *In the Company of Spies*, who visited with CIA officials to research his role as an Agency officer. In 1999, Berenger stated that the CIA deserves more credit than it is generally given, because "if they do something well and right you never hear about it."[23]

Admittedly, the White House has often used the CIA as a scapegoat when operations go wrong, even though the executive branch must approve the CIA's covert operations. For operational reasons, the CIA's successes must also stay a secret if the same methods are to be used in the future. Nonetheless, the CIA's "company motto" is conveniently impossible to disprove, since it allows the Agency to claim that it regularly averts national threats without the organization ever having to disclose the threat level of those attacks, the frequency of these successes, or even the veracity of the claim at all. Nonetheless, *The Recruit's* coproducer Roger Birnbaum echoed the CIA's favorite talking point in interviews he did to promote the film, demonstrating the degree to which Brandon and the CIA were able to influence (or at least reinforce) the filmmakers' public perspective on the Agency. For example, when asked what he hoped audience members would learn from his movie, Birnbaum responded that "the CIA operatives in this country and around the world are here to protect us and it's a very difficult job. Usually the American public only hears about their mistakes. We don't get to hear about the great things they do every day. It's only when they stumble do we hear about it. But probably even right now, as you and I are standing here about to enjoy this movie, someone is out there doing something good that we'll never know about."[24] Given that Birnbaum and Apple credit Brandon with shaping their understanding of the Agency, this sentiment was very likely the successful result of the CIA's public relations campaign, and basically asked viewers to cut the Agency some slack by hinting that its recent errors regarding the 9/11 attacks are not the norm.

In addition to curtailing the criticism that the CIA was ill prepared for 9/11, other aspects of *The Recruit* helped the CIA further burnish its image. Of the recruits who train at The Farm, for example, several are multilingual, with Farsi being the language highlighted. Farrell's character grew up overseas in Uzbekistan, Venezuela, and Brunei; Moore is supposedly half Algerian and half French; and the film's extras stem from multiple racial backgrounds. These details all projected an image of a CIA that is strong in relevant language programs and drawn from a greater diversity of recruits, thus curtailing one of the specific criticisms launched at the Agency in *The 9/11 Report*. Again, these details helped the Agency project a public image that suggested it was no longer stuck in a Cold War mode, but instead was ready and able to fight the new war on terror. These scenes also let viewers know what kinds of skills the CIA is now looking for, helping the Agency to more accurately recruit a certain kind of applicant. (In fact, one recruit featured in the film speaks both Spanish and English but had to go back to school to learn Farsi to be accepted by the Agency. Such a detail let viewers know that the CIA does not seek out all bilingual skills.)

Additionally, the training at The Farm focuses on human intelligence — how to spot, develop, and turn an asset — helping the CIA assure viewers that the Agency is not totally focused on electronic, satellite, and signals acquisitions. In fact, the spy genre's usual focus on satellite technology, high-tech gadgetry, and electronic surveillance is largely absent from this film, which instead focuses on the basics of human tradecraft and deceit, thereby addressing the *9/11 Report*'s criticisms that the Agency was weak on human intelligence.

More generally, the film also depicts CIA officers as selfless patriots, as Burke tells his new recruits that people do not join the CIA because of the fame, the money, or because it helps them "to get laid." Rather, people join the CIA because they "believe in good and evil and choose good. Our cause is just." The film therefore helped to depict CIA officers as highly intelligent people who generously sacrifice lucrative jobs in the private sector for careers in dangerous public service. The depiction is a far cry from the image of the CIA officer as a buffoon or evil assassin that has so often been showcased in other CIA-related films.

As Harlow points out, though, *The Recruit* is not a perfect commercial for the Agency, since the second half of the film takes a more negative approach to its depiction of the CIA. In the last training exercise shown at The Farm, for instance, the CIA kidnaps Clayton, puts him in a holding cell, and subjects him to food deprivation, electroshock, and physical abuse. The point of the exercise is to drive home that "rule number one is do not get caught," but the idea that the CIA would torture its own officers would certainly be off-putting to viewers and potential recruits alike, especially those who do not believe the CIA should be torturing anyone at all. The most damaging depiction of the Agency, however, comes in the final characterization of Burke, as viewers learn that he is using Layla and James (who now work at the CIA) to steal a computer program called ICE9. Just by plugging a device into a wall and allowing the program to connect to existing, interconnected wires, this code could cripple a nation's entire power system. Burke plans to sell the program for $3 million in cash because he no longer "believes" in the Agency's mission and could no longer fake it. His disillusionment stems partially from the fact that he spent twenty-seven years "neck-deep in shit" collecting information for Langley only to be recalled from the field and told he is now irrelevant.

But even this part of the film is not a total negative from the CIA's perspective. One of the primary subtexts in the film is that CIA officers are not paid enough. Indeed, on the first day of training, Burke tells the recruits that GS-15 pay-grade officers, like himself, make only $75,000 a year—not enough "to even buy a decent sports car." Burke also tells Clayton that intelligence is an ugly business and that the government could never pay CIA officers enough for the type of work they do. Thus viewers understand that Burke also betrays the Agency to secure his financial security after retirement. As Steve Sailer astutely writes, one of the take-home messages of *The Recruit*, then, is that "while the CIA does have problems with officers committing treason, it's mostly because we don't pay them enough"—an angle Brandon would have little problem getting behind (and maybe even suggested, as a similar theme ran throughout *In the Company of Spies*).[25]

In the end, then, *The Recruit* suggests that the CIA is enlisting a new generation of highly intelligent patriots, champions salary increases for its employees, and helps reassure viewers that the Agency has the linguistic and cultural talent needed to effectively engage in human intelligence collection during the war on terror. Working at the CIA is also depicted as challenging, purposeful, and lively. Arguably, the story line of Burke's betrayal even helped mask *The Recruit*'s cooperation with the CIA's PAO, since the ending, which is mostly unfavorable to Langley, delivered a twist to viewers, and thus made the entire film appear more like a thrill ride rather than a propaganda vehicle.

But if *The Recruit* might be considered well-disguised propaganda, *The Sum of All Fears* was over the top in its positive depictions of Langley. In fact, more than any other of the Agency's post-9/11 projects, this film was the most unabashedly celebratory of the CIA, helping the Agency to again curtail criticisms in the wake of 9/11. It was also the most successful CIA-assisted film to date. Debuting in 2002, this film earned $118 million in its domestic release alone, and a little shy of $200 million worldwide. While

The Recruit's modest commercial success suggests that its potential to influence viewers' opinions of the Agency was significant, the reach of *The Sum of All Fears* was undoubtedly greater.

The Sum of All Fears

There have been four adaptations of Tom Clancy's novels featuring his CIA hero Jack Ryan. The first, *The Hunt for Red October*, debuted in 1990, followed by *Patriot Games* (1992), *Clear and Present Danger* (1994), and *The Sum of All Fears* (2002). These films have been among the most positive depictions of the Agency in cinematic history, especially as they relate to Ryan and CIA helmsmen, James Greer and William Cabot, all of whom have been constructed as highly competent, ethical, and patriotic.[26]

Within the franchise, however, *The Sum of All Fears* is undoubtedly the most positive in its depiction of the Agency, and unsurprisingly, it was the only installment that received full CIA cooperation.[27] For instance, the CIA welcomed Ben Affleck (Jack Ryan) to headquarters, where he spent roughly three days working with the CIA's Russian analysts to better understand his character. Affleck and the film's director, Phil Alden Robinson, also met with DCI George Tenet and other high-ranking officials, who offered their insights into the CIA's mission and operations. The film's set designers were also invited to campus to get a feel for the layout of the building, including its operations center, and the filmmakers were allowed to shoot some aerials over the campus and some other exterior scenes.

Chase Brandon also went out of his way to assist the film with props. For instance, when he learned that the CIA had some badge machines that were broken, he arranged to have them shipped to the set in Montreal to be used during filming (though at the filmmakers' expense).[28] Likewise, Brandon took unclassified material from bulletin boards and desks in Langley so the filmmakers could replicate the Agency's Russia desk, down to the scraps of paper.[29] Brandon also served as an on-set adviser for the film, and the director of public relations, Bill Harlow, accompanied him on occasion. Brandon also appears in a special feature of the film's DVD in which he touts the film's realism.

Unfortunately, no public information exists about how the CIA was able to negotiate these services for influence over the evolving script, but it is clear that the final product depicts the CIA in a very heroic light. Further, Paramount Pictures publicly embraced Brandon, whom it used to market the film as a timely, serious critique of world relations, rather than as an exploitative, summer blockbuster debuting shortly after 9/11.

Regarding the film's flattering portrayal of the CIA, consider that in *The Sum of All Fears*, the inner-agency nemesis common to other Jack Ryan films is completely absent.[30] Instead, the only threats to American national security are a neo-Nazi terrorist group and the president's hotheaded security advisers, who want to drop nuclear weapons on the Russians without strong evidence of their guilt. Additionally, while in previous Jack Ryan adaptations the filmmakers added negative elements regarding the CIA that were not present in the original novel, *The Sum of All Fears* reversed that trend through the character of Director Cabot. In Clancy's novel of the same name, Cabot is an inept political appointee, largely incapable of heading the CIA. He also plays little role in resolving the book's crisis. In the movie, however, Cabot is a highly competent leader and an excellent adviser to the president and his staff. Throughout the film, Cabot makes it clear that he wants to provide accurate information, stressing to Ryan that he should never give advice about a topic with which he is unfamiliar, and that he should never be afraid to say that he does not know an answer. Words have a habit of becoming policy, Cabot states, so the CIA's advice to the president and to Congress must be weighed carefully.

Additionally, the film features the CIA as extremely competent in intelligence analysis through the character of Ryan. The story focuses on a neo-Nazi terrorist group intent on destroying Russia and the United States in order to give smaller nations greater autonomy and power. The group carries out a number of strikes against both countries, making it appear as if each behemoth is attacking the other. Tensions are greatly increased when the group detonates a nuclear bomb in Baltimore, almost killing the president and successfully killing the director of the CIA (played by Morgan Freeman) along with numerous other citizens. As the terrorists hoped, the U.S. president believes the bomb is the work of the Russian state and threatens to launch a nuclear attack in retaliation, thereby inviting an atomic holocaust. That dire fate is averted due to the almost single-handed efforts of the young Jack Ryan. His sharp analysis of the Russian president's personality leads him to correctly suspect that Alexander Nemerov is not responsible for the escalating tensions or the blast. During an inspection of a Russian nuclear facility, Ryan also notices that a small group of scientists are missing from the premises, an insight that later leads the CIA to learn that those men are making a bomb for the terrorist group. Ryan is also able to track down the origin of the bomb material once it has exploded, allowing him to prove that the Russians were not responsible. And at the end of the film, just before nuclear war threatens to ensue, Ryan is able to convince the Russian president to agree to a stand-down, and he ultimately convinces the U.S. president of Nemerov's innocence.

Just like *The Recruit*, images in *The Sum of All Fears* helped the CIA bolster its image during a wave of public criticism after 9/11. The depiction of Cabot, for instance, helped counter the idea that the DCI was unable to lead the intelligence community and serve as chief adviser to the president. Indeed, Cabot is one of the wisest, most even-keeled characters in the whole film, and he performs all his functions, especially his role as presidential and congressional adviser, particularly well. This sentiment was echoed by the film critic Mick LaSalle, who noted in the *San Francisco Chronicle* that "the real wise men in *The Sum of All Fears* aren't the politicians but the professionals, who think before they act and know what they're going to say before they say it." LaSalle argues that this is particularly well illustrated by Freeman's performance, as Cabot continually projects the aura "of a man in a world of boys," which includes various member of Congress, the president, and his security advisers.

Additionally, while the film plays on old Cold War paranoias, it nonetheless constructs the CIA as the only agency thinking outside of the U.S.-Soviet paradigm. It recognizes that global terrorist cells now pose more of a threat than traditional U.S.-Russian relations, and thus undermines the idea that the CIA was operating under an outdated psychological structure. Likewise, by featuring Ryan as a sharp member of the Directorate of Intelligence, the film helped counter criticisms that the CIA lacked a strong intelligence analysis capability.

Of course, there is no way the CIA could have known just how timely the film's images would be, given that the producers had completed filming a few months before 9/11 took place. Originally, the CIA's decision to support the film likely mirrored the navy's when it agreed to assist *The Hunt for Red October*. Because of the popularity of this Clancy novel and the anticipated popularity of the motion picture, the navy claimed that it expected a "heightened interest in its submarine program,"[31] and that the film would help provide "a positive portrayal of the professionalism and personal excellence of Navy people."[32] The CIA, too, hoped *The Sum of All Fears* would generate interest in the Agency and highlight (indeed, exaggerate) the "excellence" of its officers. Further, in featuring a third-party threat, it most likely looked to the film to reassure viewers about the need for the Agency after the collapse of the Soviet Union.

With its release less than a year after 9/11, however, *The Sum of All Fears* and its focus on European terrorists with nuclear capabilities must have resonated differently with viewers than the producers originally envisioned. For instance, *New York Magazine*'s Peter Rainer argued that *The Sum of All Fears*, despite its solid craftsmanship, was simply "upstaged by the sum of *our* fears. The staunch heroics, frantic presidential huddles, and hairbreadth rescues," he writes, "all seem tinny and escapist, too Cold Warrior–ish, for what's really going on now."[33] Likewise, LaSalle stated that "the picture, which turns on a cataclysmic act of terrorism within U.S. borders, was made for a different audience from the one that's about to see it. It was made for an audience who could watch it at a cozy remove and be vicariously thrilled at the sight of America being attacked."[34] That audience no longer existed, and thus La Salle claims that the film, although well made, offers "neither escape nor edification and that at times is just hard to watch."

Part of the reason the film was "just hard to watch" is the glibness with which it treats the destruction caused by the Baltimore attack. Ryan's girlfriend, for instance, who works in a nearby hospital is untouched by the bomb. While the explosion causes Ryan's helicopter to drop out of the sky, he miraculously walks away from the wreckage only to highjack a car and survive another crash in his pursuit to investigate the bombing. Likewise, the president survives even though his motorcade is blown off the road, and there's no hint that he will suffer from radiation exposure. And while Cabot dies in the attack, it is a quiet, clean, noble, and seemingly painless exit. These neat images simply could not be enjoyed at a distance given the reality and proximity of 9/11, where people jumped out of the World Trade Center rather than be consumed by fire, were crushed under beams of steel, or simply incinerated, and the effects on these victims' families were still being explored in public discourse.

Anticipating the criticism that *The Sum of All Fears* would seem more exploitative than entertaining, Paramount Pictures launched a media campaign to shift critics' perspectives of the film. For instance, Paramount screened rough cuts of the movie for reviewers before its release, where they encouraged writers to see the film as a cautionary tale with a high purpose. Salon.com's Charles Taylor argues that these attempts were successful, as many of his colleagues indeed treated the film as a "cautionary tale along the lines of *Fail-Safe* or *Seven Days in May*," even though he remained unconvinced.[35] One of the ways Paramount accomplished this was by stressing its relationship with the CIA during the preproduction and production stages to endow the film with a sense of authenticity and relevance.

For instance, in a press packet circulated by Paramount Pictures, Chase Brandon was asked if he thought the film's basic premise was realistic. He responded that he did, but he specifically argued that during the Cold War era, the CIA "was legitimately focused on one monolithic threat, the Soviet military. . . . Now that the Cold War is over, there's a new world order," he stated, "and instead of a giant dragon, we have a jungle full of venomous snakes, from the proliferation of weapons of mass destruction . . . to rogue nation states."[36] This shift, he argued, had "made the agency more consequential than ever," and he claimed that because the film stressed that concept, *The Sum of All Fears* was characterized by "remarkable accuracy and drama."[37] Brandon also claimed that the film's depiction of a new world order accurately demonstrates that "angry, frustrated, intelligent people could find many ways—from low-tech to high-tech—to inflict damage on this country and throw our economy into a tailspin,"[38] and again he argued that the Agency, as a result, was needed more than ever before.

Brandon's comments, and others like them, reflect the mutually beneficial relationship that the CIA and Hollywood enjoy. Brandon's statements helped Paramount pitch the film as an "authentic" look at the CIA, as a serious commentary on U.S. foreign affairs, and as a cautionary tale about the continued need for a strong intelligence community. Indeed, in his review, Charles Taylor even claimed that while *The Sum of All Fears* was both implausible and exploitative, the fact that the movie's solution to averting terrorist threats "is more and better intelligence" gave the film "more cachet." Recent headlines regarding the failure of our national intelligence organizations, he stated, made the film's real-life connections and commentary "impossible to deny."[39] Brandon's suggestion that the film tapped into the fear that unconventional and catastrophic attacks would continue to occur on U.S. soil were also echoed by famed film critic Roger Ebert, who summarized that "in these dark times," *The Sum of All Fears* "is not a thriller but a confirmer, confirming our fears that the world is headed for disaster."[40]

But Brandon's public embrace by Paramount also helped the CIA stress the need for continued financial and public support, as Brandon encouraged viewers to see *The Sum of All Fears* as a film that warns viewers about living in a world without reliable intelligence agencies. Brandon also used his connections with Paramount to publicly attempt to get viewers to see

the film as embodying "the heroism and intelligence and bravery and dedication and patriotism of the actual Jack and Jill Ryans who work in the
agency as analysts."[41] Most important, however, Brandon's public comments made explicit what the film made implicit: the idea that the CIA
was needed now more than ever, without ever commenting on the problems that had plagued the Agency in the months leading up to 9/11 and
how they might still need attention. These examples all illustrate that the
CIA's cooperation on *The Sum of All Fears* not only provided the CIA with
the chance to influence the image of the Agency within the film, but also
a chance to influence the conversation surrounding the release and how
that conversation might influence viewers' and critics' reading of the film.

"Terrorists Watch TV, Too": Technology and Intimidation

As is obvious from the above sections, both *The Sum of All Fears* and
The Recruit depicted the CIA in a favorable light and were highly supported by the Agency. By emphasizing Langley's language capabilities,
its strengths in analysis, the wisdom of the DCI, and the Agency's ability
to move past a Cold War paradigm, these films helped counter some of
the criticisms circulating about the CIA in the aftermath of 9/11. But the
CIA has benefited from its ability to shape its image within Hollywood
in another way as well.

One of the reasons that filmmakers often consult with CIA officers
is to learn about the Agency's technological capabilities in order to enhance the accuracy, or at least the realism, of their texts. According to
John Strauchs, when the screenwriter Lawrence Lasker was lambasted by
a group in Silicon Valley for the technological absurdity of *War Games*
(1983), he was determined to avoid similar criticisms of *Sneakers* (1992),
and thus worked with the former CIA officer John Strauchs to endow the
film with a sense of realism.[42] Likewise, the creators of *Enemy of the State*
approached the CIA to learn about the intelligence community's surveillance technology and were granted access to Langley's archives and the
assistant director. More recently, the staff of *Alias* courted the CIA for
technical guidance since they regularly featured Bond-like gadgetry in
their series. Chase Brandon reportedly briefed them on "declassified technology" to provide a "foundation of what our equipment and our capability—technologically speaking—look like."[43] Brandon also assisted the
filmmakers of *The Recruit* by approving "the veracity of certain gadgets
and types of technology used in the film."[44]

While this type of collaboration seems merely technical in nature, it is important to realize that the CIA, and even its retired officers, are rarely interested in providing accurate information to filmmakers when it comes to current technology—sometimes with good reason. Before agreeing to work on *Sneakers*, for instance, Strauchs made it clear that he did not want to "create a training video for would-be criminals."[45] Therefore, he and the director agreed that Strauchs would help create "a totally inaccurate" film, just "in a highly sophisticated way." A good example, he stated, was a scene in *Sneakers* where Robert Redford's character is going to break into a room that has a sensor to detect body heat. In order to prevent Redford from being detected, the team increases the indoor temperature to 98.6 degrees. But 98.6 degrees is a human's internal body temperature, not its external temperature, which hovers around 89 or 90 degrees, and thus the plot would not work in real life. Viewers rarely detect this type of misdirection, so it still works to increase the realism of the film, but not its technical accuracy.

Like Strauchs, the CIA also recognizes that would-be criminals and would-be terrorists consume American media, and therefore the Agency is invested in keeping its actual technological capacities secret. In fact, Chase Brandon noted that while he would help "fair and balanced" filmmakers depicting the Agency, he would not reveal the CIA's secrets, methods, or sources.[46] This does not mean, however, that the CIA is uninterested in using film and television to impress its power on evildoers through an exaggerated depiction of the Agency's capabilities. As the previous chapter demonstrates, Chase Brandon worked with Michael Frost Beckner on *The Agency* in order to increase the authenticity of the show, but he also pitched at least one fictionalized story line that would intimidate terrorists because, as he told Beckner, "terrorists watch TV, too."[47] This idea involved a highly futuristic biometric device that could detect terrorists in airports. Brandon admitted that the device was not real, but he argued that Beckner should put it in the show anyway because it would make for a good scare tactic.

While it is not clear whether the CIA has so explicitly pitched scare tactics to other writers, it is clear that the Agency serves as a major source of technical information for many producers, and these texts all depict American intelligence as highly advanced in regard to its surveillance and communication powers. Season 1 of *Alias*, for instance, features thermal sunglasses that can see behind walls, a phone disguising a biometric sensor with a fingerprint-scanning digitizer, sunglasses that contain a high-resolution retina scanner, a ring that detects heartbeat signatures, and nonlethal radioactive isotopes that can be ingested and then tracked by geosynchronous satellites. Likewise, *Mission: Impossible* (1996) featured Ethan Hunt (Tom Cruise) breaking into the CIA in order to download a nonofficial cover list from the headquarters mainframe. The security depicted inside Langley is formidable, as the list is held in a room with a single terminal connected to an isolated computer, which is monitored by an operator at almost all times. Whenever the operator must leave the room, the floor becomes pressure sensitive, the room becomes heat sensitive, and even the slightest sound will trigger an alarm. Even *In the Company of Spies*, a decidedly non-glossy spy film, features a voice simulator that transforms a CIA officer's voice into one that sounds exactly like a terrorist's contact. As the CIA historian Nicholas Dujmovic states, this kind of technology would likely not have been realistic at the time because "any technology which, if real, would be very sensitive and therefore presumably unknown to filmmakers." Nonetheless, he stated that "speaking personally, I would like every terrorist in the world to have doubts when he's really speaking to his terrorist colleagues."[48] CIA technical advisers likely share Dujmovic's perspective, and thus if they cannot share accurate technology for security reasons, it makes sense for them to pitch ideas that exaggerate the Agency's capabilities rather than have filmmakers depict Langley as using merely average or even outdated technology.

Indeed, the construction of the CIA as a highly effective surveillance and security outfit is reinforced not just by the films it assists; it is also accomplished in the press material for these texts. For instance, in a release for *Enemy of the State*, Will Smith claimed that the CIA's technology is "astounding"; through his research at the Agency, he discovered that the CIA developed computers that could tell what someone was typing just from the sound, and it possessed cameras hidden in toothpicks. But these things "were old, things they don't use anymore!"[49] Smith also claimed that viewers "have to imagine that anything [they] see in a movie today is probably 10 to 15 years behind what the government actually has."[50] Given that *Enemy of the State* projected the American intelligence community (and primarily the National Security Agency) as capable of using a satellite to home in on someone's block, transmit images from a person's living room to anyone in the world with the right technology, record moving images with satellites, and mine databases for the most personal of details, the comment was formidable.

Yet, in some ways, the claim is accurate. As Peter Earnest, the director of the International Spy Museum in Washington, DC, points out, overhead satellites, document scanners, and even the Internet were all developed and used by government agencies before they were available on the commercial market.[51] That does not mean, however, that spy films are always ahead of the times when it comes to an outfit's technological capacities. Tony Scott (the director of *Enemy of the State*) admitted that the CIA did not have the ability to record moving images with satellites, and *Patriot Games* featured satellites that could give real-time, close-up video of events on the ground—something that Director James Woolsey "found funny."[52] Indeed, the CIA has even taken inspiration from Hollywood. According to Earnest, the 1960s television program *Mission: Impossible* prompted numerous operatives to "run into the OTS [Office of Technical Services] to see if they could get their hands on some device they had seen in an episode," while Tony Mendez explains that CIA leadership began to develop facial-recognition software only after it was featured in the James Bond film *A View to a Kill* (1985). And even though the CIA does have powerful signals-collection methods, that does not mean it has the staff to translate every conversation or analyze every photograph a satellite takes—a fact that is rarely, if ever, featured in Hollywood productions. Likewise, while spy agencies are able to track personal activities and interests through databases and credit card purchases, the process is not as instantaneous as films suggest.

Therefore, even though Smith's claim is not totally inaccurate, it does hint at how spy films and television shows have encouraged viewers to see the CIA and the NSA as more omnipresent and omnipotent than they really are. Mark Bowden, author of *Black Hawk Down*, and Director of Operations Bill Daugherty (who was also taken hostage in Iran), shared one example of how these images have real-life consequences. During the 1970s hostage crisis in Tehran, they explained, the Iranians often worried that the American embassy workers' watches were really CIA communication devices and that hostages could flag Langley down simply by waving at the sky to attract one of their satellite's attention. (On one occasion, an American hostage even decided "to play" with the hostage takers by waving wildly at the sky when he was let outside for exercise, much to the Iranians' horror.) The Iranians also believed that the CIA controlled the weather and could cause earthquakes. All these ideas, according to Daugherty and Bowden, stemmed from the Iranians watching too many spy films that featured high-tech gadgetry and the CIA as an omnipotent and omnipresent power.[53]

Of course, high-tech gadgetry has been a staple of the spy genre since the introduction of the James Bond franchise, and thus the CIA is not solely responsible for its all-powerful image. Nonetheless, it has worked to continue that image in CIA-assisted texts, where the Agency's official association encourages viewers to see those images of a technologically advanced organization as accurate — and sometimes the Agency itself even suggests exaggerated technology.

Maintaining and Creating Contacts

Finally, one of the other benefits stemming from the CIA's decision to work with filmmakers is that the practice allows the Agency to establish powerful contacts that may prove useful on future collaborations. Indeed, in 2007, the CIA attorney John Rizzo explained that the CIA has "a very active" network of people in Hollywood helping "in whatever way they can to give back."[54] Rizzo did not explain the exact nature of these people's assistance, but it includes boosting internal morale, volunteering to depict the Agency and its policies in a favorable light, and, on rare occasions, engaging in covert action on its behalf.

Regarding the boosting of internal morale, consider that when Mike Myers, Kevin Bacon, and Michael Bacon visited Langley in 2009 to take a personal tour, the celebrities stopped to sign autographs and take photographs with employees and expressed their gratitude for the CIA's work. The Bacon brothers stated that while "we don't know exactly what you people do . . . we're really glad you're doing it,"[55] while Myers, star of the *Austin Powers* spy spoofs, told several hundred CIA officers how "grateful" he is for their service.[56] In the spring of 2010, an Agency spokeswoman said that the CIA was also in the process of arranging for the stars of a current and "highly popular" television series to visit the campus in order to "do a little flag waving."[57] (Those actors were almost certainly from *24*, since the CIA had assisted this program at one time and the CIA spokeswoman had not heard of *Chuck*, the other major spy show on at the time.)

Since the director of the CIA and representatives from its media relations team often meet with celebrity visitors, who are either working on projects or are simply interested in taking a tour, these interactions may encourage celebrities to consult or collaborate with the CIA on future projects as well. Indeed, this was one of the main reasons that Chase Brandon and Bill Harlow served as on-set advisers to films when they could. According to Harlow, their presence was more about taking advantage of important networking opportunities than performing a supervisory role. "We thought it was a good idea to continue to build relationships with the people around [a] film," he said, as "we wanted to maintain ties with those people when they went off to work with other projects."[58] Because Hollywood creators often work within the same genre, this strategy makes sense. After all, the brothers Roger and Robert Towne have independently written *In the Company of Spies*, *The Recruit*, *Mission: Impossible*, and *Mission: Impossible II* (2000), while Robert Towne has another spy thriller, *The 39 Steps*, in development. Likewise, Mace Neufeld's company has produced each of the Tom Clancy/Jack Ryan films to date, including *The Sum of All Fears*; Michael Frost Beckner wrote both *Spy Game (2001)* and *The Agency*; J. J. Abrams produced *Alias* and directed *Mission: Impossible III* (2006), while Paul Attanasio, writer of *The Sum of All Fears*, later went on to write *The Good German* (2006), and currently has a Matt Helm project in development. Doug Liman, who directed *The Bourne Identity* (2002), *Mr. and Mrs. Smith* (2005), and *Fair Game* (2010), is also the executive producer of USA's *Covert Affairs* (2010–). By creating and maintaining a good relationship with filmmakers on set or during Langley visits, then, the chances are good that the CIA will have another opportunity to influence the content and tone of future productions. Indeed, Doug Liman stated that much of the "treasure trove" of information he garnered from the CIA during his research for *Fair Game* made its way into the spy series *Covert Affairs*,[59] and the contacts he developed while working on *Fair Game* also helped secure a CIA visit for Piper Perabo when she was studying for her starring TV role as Annie Walker.[60]

Finally, on rare occasions, the CIA's relationship with Hollywood insiders may also prove useful to intelligence gathering or covert operations. Michael Sands, for instance, used his Hollywood contacts to help Paul Barry meet studio heads and powerful theatrical agents (see chapter 2), but because he also works as a celebrity publicist, he has been able to use his connections to assist ongoing investigations. One such case was that of Abu Abbas, the mastermind behind the highjacking of the *Achille Lauro* cruise ship in 1985. According to Sands, he used his media company to convince Abbas that he was interested in "doing his book and movie," and then used his contacts with Finnish filmmakers to arrange for a five-hour interview with the terrorist. That interview took place in Baghdad on August 13, 2001, for a movie called *Portrait of a Terrorist*. As soon as the filming was over, however, Sands sent a copy of the interview, as well as Abbas's cell phone and fax number, to the FBI and the CIA. Sands believes this information helped the government eventually track and capture Abbas, who was finally arrested in the spring of 2003.[61]

While Sands's relationship with both Hollywood and the intelligence community is unique (Sands often appears on E!, has represented Britney Spears's ex-husband Kevin Federline, *and* works as a DOD contractor), his story nonetheless presents a model for how Hollywood insiders can be useful in government operations, much like the story of Studio Six Productions described in the introduction of this book. For this covert operation, the famous makeup artists John Chambers and Bob Sidell helped Langley create a front film company that pretended to be working on a picture set in Iran. The project was designed to provide covers for six American embassy workers trapped inside the country during the hostage crisis of the 1970s, and they would eventually pose as a group of Canadians who had just scouted the country for shooting locations and transportation logistics in order to pass through Iranian customs and safely return to the United States.

Conclusion

As each of these categories illustrates, the CIA's relationship with the Hollywood community provides the Agency with numerous benefits. These range from helping recruitment to deflecting criticism, from exaggerating its technological capabilities to boosting internal morale and even receiving assistance in intelligence operations. But the CIA's relationship with the motion picture industry also presents a number of ethical and legal quandaries that the CIA has tried to suppress. These issues are fully explored in the next chapter of this book, which specifically examines questions of the First Amendment and the use of propaganda in a democracy.

CHAPTER 5

The Legal and Ethical Implications of the CIA in Hollywood

The CIA has formally worked with the motion picture industry for over fifteen years. The prior chapters of this book have largely focused on the ends and the means of that involvement. The CIA's particular relationship with Hollywood, however, also raises several legal and ethical concerns, especially since the Agency refuses to assist any filmmaker depicting it in an unfavorable light. By exploring these issues in detail, this chapter ultimately concludes that the CIA's refusal to support all filmmakers seeking its assistance constitutes a violation of free speech. It also posits that the CIA's efforts to influence texts should be defined as propaganda, rather than the educational initiatives Langley claims them to be. This chapter also argues that Langley's actions violate the spirit, and perhaps even the letter, of the publicity and propaganda laws, which forbid the government from engaging in self-aggrandizing and covert communication.

First Amendment Rights to Free Speech

In *Operation Hollywood*, David Robb explains that filmmakers often seek Pentagon assistance during production since the government is able to provide submarines, aircraft carriers, helicopters, and tanks at little or no cost to the studio or production company. The Pentagon welcomes these requests because it provides them the opportunity to leverage its very expensive equipment to get filmmakers to change dialogue and delete scenes that portray the military unfavorably. If the filmmakers refuse to meet its demands, the Pentagon simply refuses to assist the project—it takes its toys and goes home.

The famed First Amendment lawyer Floyd Abrams[1] argues that the Pentagon's actions violate filmmakers' rights to free speech. He explains that there are two suspect types of limitations on free speech. The first involves limitations based on the subject being discussed, and his example is simple: The army cannot say that it doesn't want any movies made about the army and then work to prohibit all films revolving around that subject matter.[2] The second involves a limitation on speech based on the viewpoint expressed by the speaker. The First Amendment has long been interpreted to mean that the government cannot use its resources to favor one type of speech over another. Thus, "if the army says we will cooperate with some filmmakers, but only ones which please us because of the position [they take] about the armed forces," that position is "even more clearly unconstitutional."[3]

The esteemed former University of Southern California law professor Erwin Chemerinsky agrees. In *Operation Hollywood*, Chemerinsky asserts that "the Supreme Court has said that above all, the First Amendment means that the government cannot participate in viewpoint discrimination."[4] It "cannot favor some speech due to its viewpoint and disfavor another because of its viewpoint." Moreover, Supreme Court Justice Anthony Kennedy wrote in his 1995 decision *Rosenberger v. The University of Virginia* that the government must abstain from "regulating speech when the specific motivating ideology or the opinion or perspective of the speaker is the rationale for the restriction."[5] Certainly, this law applies to the CIA just as it does the Pentagon. Therefore, Langley's refusal to help some filmmakers because of their depictions of the CIA while supporting other filmmakers because of their (differing) viewpoints is a breach of the First Amendment.

As evidence that the CIA refuses cooperation with some filmmakers, consider that in 2007 Paul Barry denied assistance to a film (most likely *Body of Lies*, released in 2008) because the original screenplay suggested that CIA officers use drugs and kill their own assets.[6] Barry specifically explained that the film's crew was seeking permission to use a number of items from the CIA, such as clocks and lighters, bearing the protected CIA seal. Before providing that consent, Barry requested to review the script. "Unfortunately," he stated, "my enthusiasm waned when I realized that the screenplay introduced a number of negative scenes, which were not in the book [on which the film was based]":

> For instance, in the very first scene an Area Division Chief was depicted as smoking hash from a pipe in his home. Later in the screenplay, a ter-

rorist informer is executed by a CIA officer instead of the book's description of terrorists killing one of their own after discovering he was working with the Americans. . . . It became pretty obvious that the writers had a particular point of view that was unfavorable to the Agency. I asked the studio to change the scenes, and they refused [so] they did not get the props they were looking for.

Chase Brandon denied assistance to *The Bourne Identity* (2002) for similar reasons, noting that the script was an "ugly" and "egregious misrepresentation" of the Agency's work,[7] and that "by page 25, [he] lost track of how many rogue operatives had assassinated people," and thus "chucked the thing in the burn bag."[8] Michael Frost Beckner asserts that the CIA also withdrew its offer of assistance to *Spy Game* (2001) after the studio and the screenwriter David Arata reworked elements of his script.[9] These revisions primarily involved the addition of the film's opening scene, in which a group of rogue CIA operatives pose as international aid doctors (which the CIA is not encouraged to do) in order to break into a prison. Chase Brandon, though, claimed that he did not support the film because when he saw the final rewrite of the script, "it had taken a turn for the worse. It showed our senior management in an insensitive light, and we just wouldn't be a part of that kind of project."[10] Indeed, *Spy Game* does depict CIA leadership unfavorably, as the group works to justify letting the Chinese execute one of its own officers in order to ensure that a new U.S.-Chinese trade agreement goes through.

The refusals of assistance to these projects stemmed from the filmmakers' depictions of the CIA, which the Agency considered to be unfavorable, and thus violate the First Amendment. Even Chase Brandon has stated that "if someone wants to slander us, it's not in our interest to cooperate."[11] But the CIA's Public Affairs Office denies that its actions are illegal. In 2008, for instance, Barry argued that free speech is *not* abridged by the CIA's refusal to provide government resources in support of a film project:

When a filmmaker requests resource assistance from the government, the terms of acceptance are negotiated. The government preference is to work with the entertainment industry and the middle ground is almost always sought on contentious issues. Nevertheless, sometimes filmmakers are unwilling to compromise. This occurs for a variety of reasons, not the least of which is the industry's desire to produce a successful commercial enterprise. By contrast, the government's primary concern is accuracy, which is not a major consideration of most filmmakers. Because of these conflicting sets of priorities, "creative differences" occasionally result. If the differences cannot be resolved, it is merely a disagreement, not censorship or an infringement of free speech.[12]

Barry also argued that in terms of assistance to the entertainment industry, there is a key distinction: "Advice and guidance is available to everyone in the American entertainment industry, thereby supporting the notion of equal access. However, discretion is used in making decisions to provide government resources in support of a film project. A good analogy might be corporate sponsorship decisions (e.g., does the project align with corporate values?). One reason the government is judicious about endorsing projects is the potential impact on recruitment."[13]

There are numerous problems with Barry's comments. For one, the government's primary concern is not accuracy; it is with promoting a positive image of itself, as will be discussed below. Second, it is true that some filmmakers are unwilling to change their scripts in order to receive CIA assistance—which is perfectly within their constitutional rights. It is also true, however, that the CIA is unwilling to assist a project because it does not like what the screenplay suggests. And precisely because the Agency uses public resources to discriminate against some and favor others based on their opinions, the CIA's actions cannot be considered the result of a mere disagreement. They are an infringement of the First Amendment. Additionally, Barry equates the CIA's actions to corporate sponsorship decisions since it wants to associate itself only with texts that communicate the right brand image. But the government is *not* a privately held corporation, and thus it does not have the same freedom to use its resources in such a highly discriminating manner. The First Amendment applies *only* to government actions, not to those taken by private or publicly traded corporations, which are allowed to censor employees' speech and act in a discriminatory manner. Finally, it is true that advice and consultation are available to everyone (within the CIA's capacities), which would be fine if that were the only type of assistance the CIA provided filmmakers. But the Agency offers much greater forms of support to projects that depict it favorably and refuses to offer the same level of support to those that depict it unfavorably, which, again, favors particular viewpoints and thus violates the Constitution.

Interestingly, the CIA's Office of Legal Counsel seems to have been acutely aware of its entertainment program's legal violations. In 2007, the CIA attorneys John Rizzo and Paul Kelbaugh spoke at the William Mitchell College of Law in St. Paul, Minnesota. During the talk, Kelbaugh argued that one of the reasons it took so long for the CIA to assist Hollywood was the legal team's concern that "if we supported one group over another in moviemaking . . . to the benefit of one group over another, there might be a misuse of appropriated funds."[14] Thus, when the CIA received a "random request for assistance, the answer we gave, the safe answer, the ethics answer, was, well, if we do it for you, we have to do it for everyone, so we don't really care to do it [at all]."[15]

Kelbaugh goes on to explain that despite the legal team's concerns, the CIA nonetheless hired Chase Brandon as its first official entertainment liaison in 1996, and just a few years later questions of the program's legality arose again inside the Agency. More specifically, Kelbaugh claims that when headquarters received its first "exciting" request for assistance from Tim Matheson, creator of *In the Company of Spies*, the CIA was very eager to support the project.[16] As a result, Agency decision makers asked Rizzo and Kelbaugh if the CIA could indeed cooperate on the project without violating any laws. Kelbaugh concluded that it could so long as the CIA was ready to provide similar assistance to any other group that approached the Agency afterward.

As chapter 3 reveals, *In the Company of Spies* received considerable assistance from the CIA. The film's crew was allowed to shoot both exterior and interior scenes at Langley and use Agency personnel as extras. The project's writer, director, and actors also consulted with several CIA officers in Virginia to help develop their product, and the Agency even premiered the film at a red-carpet event on campus. Of course, this kind of support has not been offered to every other group that came in after *In the Company of Spies*, and the CIA has even refused to assist some of Matheson's successors altogether.[17]

It is possible, and even probable, that the CIA never resolved this issue legally, but rather looked around and realized that the Pentagon, FBI, Secret Service, and a host of other federal agencies have been working with Hollywood in a discriminatory manner for decades without repercussions. In fact, during the forum at William Mitchell College, both Rizzo and Kelbaugh evoked their predecessors' actions to explain the CIA's own decision to work with Hollywood. When discussing the decision to hire Brandon, for instance, Kelbaugh noted that the Agency now had a place where it could respond to Hollywood "just like the FBI has been doing for all of these years"; Rizzo argued that he would like to see an even deeper relationship with Hollywood, since "we are way far behind" the DOD and FBI programs. Rizzo noted, "They've gotten a lot of mileage out of cooperating with Hollywood over the years."[18]

So why have so many federal agencies been able to get away with violating the First Amendment for so long? Robb and Chemerinsky believe the reason is simple: nobody has ever sued over it. And in some ways, it is easy to see why. Filmmakers greatly benefit from the government's entertainment liaison programs, which offer sympathetic production companies stock footage, location shooting, technical consultants, extras, props, advice, and expensive equipment, all free of charge. But that doesn't explain why filmmakers fail to act when their requests are denied by the government, or even why production companies or the Writers Guild of America have failed to sue. As Robb points out, it's their members' creative freedoms that are most limited by federal agencies demanding script changes in exchange for government assistance.[19]

The answer lies in issues of practicality. For instance, most independent production companies do not have the resources — or the will — to mount and fight such a legal challenge. Presumably, major studios do have the legal resources, but they are likely more concerned about its bottom line than fighting censorship and defending free speech rights. Studios may also be leery of antagonizing the government. This would seem particularly true since the government's likely reaction to such a lawsuit would be to simply withdraw *all* support for filmmakers to avoid viewpoint discrimination. This decision would dearly cost the studios as they would need to recreate or rent their own submarines and naval carriers as well as hire their own technical consultants, military personnel, and extras. It seems that until someone decides to take on the government in the court system, federal agencies will continue to use the entertainment industry to improve their public image in an unconstitutional manner.

The Rhetoric of Authenticity; or Propaganda versus Education

Just as the government is not allowed to use its resources to favor one group over another, it is also forbidden from using appropriated funds for publicity or propaganda purposes (unless specifically authorized by Congress).[20] Historically, the Government Accountability Office has been responsible for interpreting these sets of laws. It asserts that while the government has the right to inform the public about its programs, it is forbidden from engaging in propaganda, which it defines as covert and self-aggrandizing communication.[21] More specifically, the GAO defines covert communication as agency communications that do not identify the agency as its source or are misleading about their origin. These communications go "beyond the range of acceptable agency public information activities," writes the lawyer Daniel Gordon, since source concealment makes it appear to the public that an independent party endorses the agency's position or statements.[22] Self-aggrandizing communications, also called puffery, are likewise outlawed. These types of communications emphasize the importance of an agency or one of its officials. For example, an agency would be prohibited from spending appropriated funds to issue a press release that attempted to persuade the public of its importance as a government agency.[23] Puffery might also be considered to go beyond emphasizing an agency's importance, to include an agency overstating its capabilities or accomplishments. The Justice Department's Office of Legal Counsel notes, however, that this prohibition does not apply to the dissemination of information to the public that is "necessary to the proper administration of the laws" for which an agency is responsible.[24] In other words, the government can educate people about its policies and practices, but it cannot engage in puffery.

According to Tom Armstrong, the GAO's specialist in propaganda and publicity laws, no one has ever asked his office to investigate any of the government's entertainment liaison programs.[25] The threshold question for considering the legality of these programs, he stated, would hinge on whether a government-assisted film or television series would be considered a communication of the filmmakers or the agency, and likely, he stated, it would be considered the filmmakers' since they possess the final creative say. Nonetheless, Armstrong argues that the publicity and propaganda laws provide an excellent framework for thinking about the *ethical* implications of these programs. Government agencies like the CIA use public resources to engage in propaganda (and especially puffery)—they just do it via the motion picture industry. In other words, the government's entertainment programs often violate the original intent of the publicity and propaganda laws, and perhaps even the actual laws themselves. These laws were put in place to ensure a free and open exchange of information between the government and its citizens, and to "result in more news and less 'bull' from the Federal publicity mill," as Senator Harry F. Byrd, the law's earliest sponsor, summed it up in the 1950s.[26]

But Joel Timmer, a media law professor and former lawyer at the FCC, is not so quick to dismiss the legal question. Because most viewers do not know that the CIA works to influence film content, and because the CIA is sometimes not even credited for its support in the final product, Timmer claims that the government's efforts are akin to covert communication, although admittedly they fall into the gray area between the letter and the spirit of the law.[27] Timmer's point parallels one raised in a 1987 case in which the GAO investigated the State Department's Office of Public Diplomacy for Latin America and the Caribbean for paying consultants to write op-ed pieces in support of the administration's policy on Central America. Ultimately, the State Department was found guilty of wrongdoing because it utilized "a portion of its appropriated funds to influence public opinion in the United States" *and* because, unlike the consultants, newspaper readers did not understand that the State Department was the true influence on the pieces.[28] The same can be said for federal agencies working with filmmakers. They often leverage their assets to get filmmakers to change dialogue and plot points they find distasteful, and while filmmakers understand the exchange, most viewers do not. Additionally, Timmer points out that while filmmakers are often thought to exercise total creative control over a product, they receive the government's assistance only if they exercise that control in a way that is acceptable to the organization in question. Thus the filmmakers' agency is not as powerful as it might appear upon first glance, which complicates Armstrong's argument that a film would likely be considered a purely independent, rather than government-sponsored, communication.[29]

It is clear, then, that a large gray area exists in any analysis of the government's relationship with Hollywood, but the framework provided above is important given the CIA's rhetoric regarding its involvement in the motion picture industry. More specifically, the CIA frequently stresses that its work in film and television serves to educate the public about the role of intelligence and the mission of the CIA. It also claims to increase the "accuracy" of texts. By using this rhetoric, the CIA evades the fact that its efforts amount to propaganda that is frequently self-aggrandizing and sometimes covert in nature.

To demonstrate the CIA's rhetoric, consider that Kent Harrington says he supported *The Classified Files of the CIA* because "Jack Myers wanted to do something that would be capable of *educating* the broad public about the role of intelligence, which is rarely shown in the whole proliferation of films that feature the Agency."[30] Likewise, Bill Harlow emphasized the concept of education when he explained that the CIA's involvement with Hollywood is important since "the vast majority of the American public forms its impression of the intelligence community from TV and movies." This sentiment was echoed again in 2007, when a CIA press release announced that Paul Barry had replaced Chase Brandon as its entertainment liaison, a position that is "vital . . . in explaining the Agency's national security mission to the American people."[31]

Furthering its claims to education, Agency spokespeople also stress that their assistance works to increase the accuracy of the organization's image in motion pictures. Indeed, Paul Barry asserted that when assessing a project, he is primarily concerned with whether it contains an "accurate, reasonable depiction of the Agency,"[32] while George Tenet stated that the CIA cooperates with Hollywood only to help "members of the entertainment industry willing to accurately portray the work of the intelligence community."[33] Chase Brandon used this rhetoric, too. When interviewed by the *New York Times* in 2001, he argued that the CIA had grown tired of being depicted on-screen as a nefarious organization and thus was trying to work with Hollywood to portray the agency more positively and accurately.[34] "Even though the trend is toward making programs about the agency more realistic," he complained, "there are, in fact, still writers and producers and directors who don't want to be confused by the facts. . . . They'd rather live in their own little creative make-believe world."[35]

To be fair to these men, the drive toward accuracy and education is sometimes a legitimate claim. For *The Sum of All Fears*, for example, Ben Affleck came to the CIA to talk with real CIA analysts in order to get a better understanding of the character he would be playing. Chase Brandon also helped several writers and actors understand the vernacular of CIA officers, and how handlers and assets communicate with one another in the field.[36] The PAO also fields a steady stream of calls from filmmakers seeking to replicate the CIA's physical environment, right down to the art on the walls, and works like *In The Company of Spies* and *The Agency* could also be considered educational in that they highlight the types of careers the CIA affords by featuring characters from various directorates.

At other times, however, the CIA's claims are dubious. For instance, Barry argues that he could not support a group of filmmakers because their script, which depicted the CIA assassinating someone, was unrealistic.[37] But as other parts of this book explain, the CIA has carried out several assassinations (and attempted several others) throughout its history. As recently as February 2010, the Obama administration even authorized the CIA to kill American citizens abroad who are believed to be linked to al-Qaeda or other terrorist organizations.[38] As chapter 3 explains, Chase Brandon also suggested at least one story line for an episode of *The Agency* that involved the CIA using futuristic biometrics. When the show's creator asked if the CIA actually had that capacity, Brandon stated that it did not, but quipped that the show should use the idea anyway since it would scare any terrorist who watches the series.[39]

In a case of a different nature, the Agency refused to assist the creators of *Patriot Games* (1992) because the CIA's executive director, R. M. Huffstutler, saw "no value" in assisting the production.[40] According to Kelbaugh, "When you're the number three guy [at the CIA], you get to make statements like this."[41] When *Patriot Games* debuted, however, many in the CIA were aghast to discover that the filmmakers had "done a real job with the [character of the] executive director."[42] According to Kelbaugh, its producers had hired an actor (J. E. Freeman) who looked a lot like Huffstutler and dressed him in a "bad suit, bad tie, bad shirt . . . and a really bad goatee." The movie also depicts Freeman's character as the only officer who fails to welcome Jack Ryan's return to the Agency and as the only officer who fails to exhibit a strong "can-do" attitude. This depiction apparently caused Kelbaugh and his colleagues to gasp, "Oh my God! Did you see what they did to the director?" The film's screenwriter, Peter Iliff, claims that *Patriot Games* was not trying to seek revenge for Huffstutler's refusal to assist the film, adding that the film's director, Phillip Noyce, did not care about "that kind of resentful nonsense."[43] Nonetheless, when the makers of the next Jack Ryan installment, *Clear and Present Danger*, requested CIA assistance, Kelbaugh states that the executive director agreed to enter into talks with the filmmakers.[44] As Kelbaugh tells it, this change of heart stemmed from Huffstutler's desire to be presented more positively, or to at least not experience a repeat of *Patriot Games*. The motive for getting involved in *Clear and Present Danger*, in other words, was not to educate the public about the role of intelligence, but rather to improve the personal image of the executive director himself. It was an issue of vanity, not accuracy.

At the risk of belaboring the point, the Agency's decision to support *Alias* also belies its purported devotion to accuracy and public education. *Alias*, after all, is a blend of science fiction, melodrama, and James Bond, and even Chase Brandon admitted that the show was not realistic: "Operations officers do things like that [those featured in *Alias*] but if you do it all the time—leaving a trail of exploded cars in your wake—you're not very good at your job as you shouldn't be drawing attention to yourself."[45] Nonetheless, Brandon still tried to frame the CIA's support of the program with the concept of accuracy. He specifically argued that Sydney Bristow is an accurate reflection of a CIA officer because she is "a person of great patriotism, intelligence, has excellent problem-solving abilities, speaks many languages, is dedicated and professional."

The same is true of Jason Bourne, however, since he also speaks several languages and is highly intelligent, resourceful, professional, and a "patriot" (albeit one misused by his government). In fact, Brandon even claimed in an interview on the film's extended DVD release that elements of *The Bourne Identity* were realistic.[46] Field officers, like Bourne, he stated, are trained in high-speed driving, secret writing, and weapons handling. Brandon also thought that the scene where the amnesiac Bourne tells Maria that he doesn't know who he is but that he does know the numbers on the license plates outside the restaurant they're in, that the waitress is left-handed, and that the best place to find a gun is in a nearby truck, was likewise realistic. Covert officers are, by nature, attentive to their environment and the people around them, Brandon claims.

So why did the CIA support the first season of *Alias* but not *The Bourne Identity*? In the first season of *Alias*, the main CIA officers are highly intelligent, morally upright, and regularly successful at disrupting national security threats. In *The Bourne Identity*, CIA management is a group of amoral, dispassionate men who establish a secret assassination program behind Congress's back. The first text helped bolster the desired image of the Agency; the other did not. The concept of accuracy was irrelevant to the decision.

Finally, it should be noted that if the CIA was really concerned with issues of accuracy and education, it should be able to assist filmmakers wishing to capture the realism of the CIA's recent destruction of interrogation tapes, its use of assassination, torture, and extraordinary rendition, or the fact that the government has recently outsourced much of its intelligence gathering to private security firms working abroad—but the Agency has consistently refused to assist these types of productions.[47] Indeed, former CIA officer Robert Baer remarks that the Agency could never even admit that they use "foreign governments, including those in Morocco and Tunisia, to help with rendition. . . . No one at the Agency is going to say, 'Oh, what the hell, let's just tell people the truth about rendition.' They can't."[48] As a result, the CIA's history mostly reflects the attitude that it should promote only its successes in order to serve the Agency's interest, rather than that of the public. In fact, Brandon has almost said as much. In 2004, he claimed that the CIA's involvement in motion pictures is primarily a function of "wanting to inform and educate the public that their tax money that keeps our front door open is money well-spent."[49] In other words, the CIA is interested in "educating" the public about its successes to keep public support up, but the Agency may ignore and even hide its failures.

In light of this information, it is fair to dismiss the CIA's claims that its work in Hollywood primarily constitutes educational outreach or a drive toward accuracy. Rather, its work is best assessed as government propaganda that is at times both self-aggrandizing and covert. As David Welch defines it, propaganda is "the dissemination of ideas intended to convince people to think and act in a particular way and for a particular persuasive purpose."[50] It varies from information and education in that propaganda seeks to narrow our perspectives and minds, whereas the former seek to open and extend them. David Culbert offers yet another definition of propaganda, stating that it is the "controlled dissemination of deliberately distorted notions in an effort to induce action favorable to predetermined ends or special interest groups."[51] And indeed, the Agency is deliberately attempting to disseminate a distorted and narrow image of itself in order to favorably influence the public's opinion, which can indirectly lead to an inducement of favorable action—whether that be boosting application levels, securing public support, receiving an increased budget, or intimidating would-be terrorists. Even the CIA legal counsel John Rizzo concedes that the Agency approaches Hollywood because the relationship provides "tangible benefits," which range from ameliorating "what would be an otherwise distasteful or slanderous portrait of CIA" to attracting recruits.[52]

Self-Aggrandizing Propaganda

Because the CIA has refused to produce any written correspondence between itself and filmmakers (even in response to Freedom of Information Act requests), it is hard to determine exactly how the CIA has leveraged its assets to secure favorable script changes, or worked to influence the writers' and directors' opinions of the Agency in the preproduction stage. We do know, however, that the Agency based its entertainment liaison program on the Pentagon's, which has a long, documented history of engaging in puffery, and that the CIA's actions often mirror those of the DOD. As such, it is useful to consider cases like *Independence Day* (1996) that demonstrate the self-aggrandizing nature of government-Hollywood interactions. Regarding this summer blockbuster, the Pentagon objected to Dean Devlin's script because, among other things, there were "no true military heroes" in the film. Phil Strub specifically complained that "the military appears impotent and/or inept" and "all advances in stopping aliens are [the] result of actions by civilians."[53] Until this could be rectified, Strub refused his assistance, which then caused Devlin to give David Levinson (Jeff Goldblum) a military background, to make General Grey

(Robert Loggia) a "more supportive and energized character," and to shift scenes so that the president "recaptures his military experience by leading his troops into battle."[54] Such demands surely qualify as attempts at puffery and propaganda, and while the CIA lacks the expensive equipment of the Pentagon to use as leverage, it nonetheless works toward the same ends. Indeed, the CIA has consistently supported texts that present an overly positive image of the Agency, such as *The Sum of All Fears*, *The Agency*, *In the Company of Spies*, and *Covert Affairs*, all of which work to aggrandize the Agency in some way. After all, the tagline for *The Agency* was "Now, more than ever, we need the CIA," while *The Sum of All Fears* features an intelligence analyst single-handedly saving the world from nuclear disaster after the president's national security advisers drop the ball. *In the Company of Spies* likewise features the president muttering, "When the Agency is good, it's spectacular and no one even knows!" *Covert Affairs* follows suit by depicting the Agency as master, albeit sensitive, manipulators of human assets, and features a team of technologically savvy, linguistically varied, and effective team leaders who rarely make mistakes.

Further supporting the point that the CIA has used Hollywood toward self-aggrandizing rather than educational ends, Baer argued, "I know the movies the CIA has cooperated on, and they are pro-CIA movies that aren't realistic":

> They need to recruit people and want to use films that add to the mystique of the job, but not the difficulty of it. They're nothing like *The Wire* [2002–2008], which constantly addresses the personal sacrifices that come with the job and how the problems its protagonists fight just continue on, or how the programs they're involved in are often a waste of time. I mean, if you arrest five people for selling drugs, and fifty people replace them, you start to question the purpose of your work. It's the same thing in the CIA. It's depressing when five generals are killed by a Predator drone and fifty more replace them. When the CIA starts backing films that explore those ideas, then I will believe that they're interested in reflecting reality and being authentic.[55]

Favorably distorted notions of the CIA admittedly help to attract potential field officers, who might otherwise avoid jobs that require dangerous work for moderate pay, but government agencies engage in propaganda for other reasons, too. As Noam Chomsky argues, the leaders of totalitarian states can easily control public thought because the threat of violence is always present: "You just hold a bludgeon over their heads, and if they get out of line you smash them over the head."[56] In more free and democratic societies, leaders lose that capacity. Therefore, they have to turn to the techniques of propaganda in order to control public thought and opinions: "The logic is clear. Propaganda is to democracy what the bludgeon is to a totalitarian state."[57] The primary creators of propaganda in a democracy, Chomsky continues, are the mass media and the multibillion-dollar public relations industry, whose primary goals have always been to control public thought in order to increase their bottom line, strengthen their agency, and increase their group's influence in society. These elites see propaganda and thought control as necessary, since their power is threatened when the masses question the relationships of authority or even the necessity or legitimacy of authority. When the public begins to question agenda setters, in other words, they may "no longer have the humility to submit to civil rule," so their attention must be marginalized, diverted, and controlled by those in power—or, at the very least, reduced to apathy.[58]

Chomsky's ideas about thought control are useful to an analysis of CIA-assisted texts, since the overwhelming majority of these works avoid hard-hitting questions about the CIA's recent intelligence failures, ethically suspect practices, and relationship with the White House. As John Diamond explains, throughout the 1990s, the CIA failed to gather accurate intelligence on a number of important issues, as evidenced by its failure to predict India's testing of nuclear weapons and North Korea's acquisition of ICBM technology. The CIA even failed to foresee the 1991 collapse of the Soviet Union. Instead, throughout the 1980s, the CIA continually warned the executive branch that the Soviet Union was getting stronger and that the United States was falling behind in the arms race— advice that led to the Reagan administration carrying out the largest peacetime military expansion in U.S. history.[59] Post-9/11, the CIA again provided faulty intelligence when it caved to political pressure exerted by the White House. As Diamond argues, the CIA's failure to uncover the September 11 plot led to bilateral congressional criticism, which weakened the CIA's political power during the lead-up to the Iraq War. In fact, between September 1 and October 10, 2002—the day before Congress voted to authorize a war with Iraq—the Joint Inquiry Committee held twelve hearings on 9/11 intelligence failures.[60] This climate left the CIA eager to regain some of its influence within the White House, and thus the Agency allowed itself to be pressured to publish intelligence it knew to be weak when it claimed that Saddam Hussein possessed numerous weapons of mass destruction.[61] This, of course, was not the case, and many regard the CIA's intelligence failure as one of the most consequential in its history since the faulty information helped to justify an entire war.

All these events caused some attentive followers to question the legitimacy of the CIA's authority in both the 1990s and the 2000s. The CIA, to retain its influence and power, had to engage in propaganda to manipulate the public's opinion about the Agency. Some of this came in the form of press releases and comments from the PAO, but others were certainly circulated by CIA-assisted movies and television series, in which these types of failures are never explored or even mentioned. Instead, viewers are presented with a highly efficient organization that is desperately needed to identify threats and save American lives. In fact, the only Agency-supported text that came close to examining any of the CIA's controversial actions was *24*, as it often featured torture in its story lines. In most cases, however, these episodes depicted torture as producing viable intelligence, and thus bolstered the CIA's push for the use of harsher interrogation techniques. Indeed, in season 4, episode 18 of *24*, government bureaucrats released a captured terrorist before he could be tortured because a lawyer for "Amnesty Global" shows up talking about the Geneva Conventions. As a result, lead agent Jack Bauer (Kiefer Sutherland) quits the Counter Terrorist Unit to become a private citizen in order to break the suspect's fingers one by one until he talks, a move championed by the narrative. The show's "gloves off" approach to fighting terrorism was likely appreciated by the CIA, which was working to push the legal and ethical boundaries (especially regarding torture) in the war on terror.

Covert Communication

Randal Marlin argues that propaganda is a "systemic, motivated attempt to influence the thinking and behavior of others through means that impede or circumvent a propagandee's ability to appreciate the nature of this influence."[62] Noam Chomsky believes that people can see through propaganda with effort,[63] but, as Marlin's quote reveals, "effort" must rest on a foundation of awareness and knowledge. In the case of CIA-assisted texts, such influence is sometimes hidden from media consumers. As chapter 2 points out, Brandon's film credits include *The Recruit*, *The Sum of All Fears*, *Enemy of the State*, *Bad Company*, and *In the Company of Spies*. But Brandon has also consulted with the makers of *Alias*, *Jag*, *The Agency*, the *Mission: Impossible* film series, and *24*, but he is never acknowledged as a consultant in their credits, and almost no one outside the projects' creative teams knows the real extent of his influence. For instance, Australian newspapers reported that Tom Cruise had met with CIA officials to discuss ways to present the Agency "in as positive a light as possible" for *Mission: Impossible III*,[64] and Michael Sands says that Brandon worked closely with Robert Towne,[65] who wrote the earlier *Mission: Impossible* films, but nothing more than this has come to light.

Additionally, in a handful of articles about Brandon's assistance to Hollywood, the liaison is simply identified as a retired CIA officer.[66] This title suggests that he no longer works for the Agency and is thus representing his own—rather than the Agency's—viewpoint to creators, which is false and misleading. For instance, in the "Cloak and Dagger" segment on *The Bourne Identity*'s extended edition DVD, Brandon is merely introduced as a CIA officer who has spent his "entire career" working in the clandestine services. His ten-year career as an entertainment liaison is never mentioned.

This type of obfuscation makes it difficult for viewers to identify propaganda in CIA-assisted texts, and for some reason, it is more common in this agency's collaborations than in those assisted by the Department of Defense. In Robb's analysis of film and television from the 1950s to the 1990s, for instance, he identified only one film—John Wayne's *The Green Berets* (1968)—that failed to thank the Pentagon for its support. That credit had been removed at the DOD's insistence, as it feared it would make the film too likely to be categorized as propaganda by viewers (which would be accurate) and would raise too many questions about how the DOD assisted the film with public resources. Perhaps this difference in openness stems from the CIA's covert culture, or the fact that it is often involved with motion pictures in the preproduction rather than the production stage, and thus producers do not feel as compelled to credit those officers who assisted them. Perhaps the filmmakers themselves desire to keep the relationship secret. After all, they are the ones responsible for creating program credits and properly identifying men like Brandon with labels overlaying their "talking head shots" in documentary features. Either way, the sometimes-hidden nature of the CIA's involvement in Hollywood disables viewers' ability to critically assess the ideologies presented in assisted texts, and may constitute covert communication as outlined in the publicity and propaganda laws.

Of course, it is not clear that viewers would perceive a text in a different light even if the CIA was properly credited in a film or television series, since these acknowledgments usually appear in small font near the *very* end of the scrolling text. Proper crediting seems like the very least the public should demand, though, especially since the FCC already has similar laws in place. Section 507 of the Communications Act of 1934, for instance, requires that when anyone "provides or promises to provide money, services, or other consideration" to companies producing broadcast material, "that fact must be disclosed in advance of the broadcast." Failure to disclose such payment or services is commonly referred to as "payola" and is punishable by a fine of not more than $10,000 or imprisonment for not more than one year.[67] This law was set in place to help the public critically consume media by allowing it to fully recognize both the parties who exert influence on a text and the producers' motives for depicting something or someone in a flattering light. These regulations were, in other words, designed to prevent covert propaganda and to better alert consumers to the possibility of a group's use of self-aggrandizement. The same rules should apply to government-sponsored texts as already do to corporate-sponsored ones.

Conclusion

The CIA uses several reasons to justify its relationship with Hollywood. These mostly revolve around the concepts of education, accuracy, and, on occasion, recruitment. Chase Brandon even once tried to claim that his job helped the CIA fulfill a congressional mandate. Speaking in 2002, the liaison claimed, "This is a nation driven by imagery. A lot of what we believe comes from what we see on that little screen in our living rooms and from what we see on that big screen at the multiplex. So the last several directors, including the current CIA director, want us following the congressional urgings, if not mandates, that we be as open and accountable as we can be."[68] The CIA's involvement with the motion picture industry, however, does not make the Agency more accountable and open in a meaningful way. The term accountability partly means taking responsibility for one's mistakes, but CIA-assisted texts do not present the Agency making significant errors, and the CIA refuses to support films that ask hard-hitting questions about its failures, ethics, and policies. Likewise, the primary objective of the CIA's media relations team is to increase positive awareness about the Agency. As such, they are selective about what they communicate to writers, actors, and directors—in short, they are open about their strengths and successes and quiet about the rest.

Further, the CIA's claims of openness and accountability are one way of evading the fact that since 1998, the Agency has actually been reducing its openness to the public outside the Hollywood model. As Kate Doyle explains, in 1993, DCI Woolsey testified before Congress that documents about eleven significant covert operations, all more than thirty years old, would be released for review in the spirit of openness and accountability. But by the time of George Tenet's inauguration, the CIA had managed to declassify documents on just two of those operations, and, in 1998, Tenet announced that the CIA simply did not have the resources to continue its declassification as promised and would cease to focus on documents exploring covert operations altogether.[69] The relapse into secrecy during Tenet's early years is likewise evidenced by the fact that the CIA has never released its annual budget since 1949, although in 1997 and 1998 it did release the intelligence communities' aggregate expenditures (Tenet refused to release the figure again starting in 1999). As pointed out by Steven Aftergood, director of the Federation of American Scientists' project on government secrecy, "For people who get their information from government documents, not from television and the movies, there has actually been a reduction in accountability" over the past several years, causing him to assert that the Agency was simply "going to have to do better than TV movies."[70]

Finally, it is important to state that the public receives little or no benefit from the CIA's relationship with television and the movies. The CIA gains an enhanced image, and producers are able to secure unique location shots, enjoy free consultation, and market their films as a rare insider's look into a secret organization, yet the taxpayers, who subsidize the relationship, only seem to receive more pro-government propaganda in return. As Ivan Eland of the Cato Institute points out, these government bureaucracies are basically enhancing their own reputation at taxpayer expense and "doling out subsidies to people who toe the government line."[71] What is more disturbing is that the taxpayer is actually subsidizing the government's violations of the First Amendment and the spirit, and perhaps even the letter, of the propaganda and publicity laws. Until the CIA resolves to embark on a new era of transparency, its Hollywood propaganda efforts will mostly disserve the American public by engaging in unconstitutional behavior and failing to initiate the nuanced discussion about its performance that is so necessary in a vibrant democracy.

The Last People We Want in Hollywood: The Retired CIA Officer and the Hollywood Docudrama

The CIA's Public Affairs Office, its entertainment liaisons, and its director have all worked with Hollywood to improve the Agency's image, but retired officers are also active in the industry. Bazzel Baz, Tony Mendez, and Jonna Mendez are all Agency retirees who have worked as technical consultants and associate producers, while the retired Chase Brandon has continued to consult filmmakers and pitch new television series. Likewise, John Strauchs served as a technical consultant on *Sneakers* (1992) and the late F. Mark Wyatt reportedly helped raise funds and circulate early prints of *Yuri Nosenko, KGB* (1986) to help generate interest in the TV movie starring Tommy Lee Jones. A host of other retirees also lend their insights to writers and directors or shop their memoirs and novels to studios.

These retirees, unlike current CIA representatives, have no obligation to provide a positive, or even fair, image of the Agency. Further, there is no way to prevent them from representing themselves as more knowledgeable than they actually are, or from attempting to settle old scores with Langley. For these reasons, the CIA has been often critical of movies and TV programs produced in collaboration with former CIA officers, as best showcased by the work of Robert Baer and Milt Bearden. Undoubtedly two of the most successful retirees in Hollywood, Baer and Bearden have provided assistance to *Meet the Parents* (2000), *Rendition* (2007), *Charlie Wilson's War* (2007), *Red* (2010), and a host of documentaries; however, their most extensive work is showcased in two Hollywood docudramas, *Syriana* (2005) and *The Good Shepherd* (2006). These post-9/11 films provide a specific framework for discussing the role of the retired CIA officer in Hollywood, why the CIA often disapproves of their involvement in the industry, and the peculiar concerns and frustrations the docudrama presents for the Agency.

The Role of the Retired CIA Officer in Hollywood

The retired officer in Hollywood plays a profoundly different role from that of the CIA's entertainment liaison. In general, this liaison can offer assistance to preproduction and production teams in the form of access to technical consultants, the D/CIA, the Agency seal, stock footage, props, shooting locations, and even Agency personnel as extras—all at little to no charge. But before agreeing to provide these services, the liaison reviews each script to ensure that it presents the Agency in a positive light and will not undermine morale or jeopardize recruitment efforts. If he or she does not think the script meets these requirements, the liaison will refuse to offer the artist assistance.

Retired CIA personnel can also offer technical consulting, but they charge for their services and any expenses they incur on the project. But retirees are not restricted in the types of projects they can support. They can—and often have—consulted on texts that disparage or criticize the CIA, and this freedom is key to many in the Hollywood community. As Bazzel Baz explains, retired personnel have "the ability to marry fantasy and fact and to be loose enough with reality to make a program entertaining."[1] Hollywood knows that the CIA has a representative, he said, but they often do not want to make a spy movie that obligates them to Langley. They do not want to send their scripts over for approval because they do not want "to be told what they can and can't do by the government." Baer put the distinction this way: people who used to work for the CIA and who do not have any government contracts can offer "an unvarnished view" of the CIA.[2] "If someone works in the CIA's media office and picks up a script that is anti-CIA," he noted, "they do not have the imagination to help that script; they only want to work on pro-CIA movies. Hollywood . . . wants conspiracies and vast corruption to add to their dramatic art. The government doesn't get that. They want CIA movies to be like old World War II films, where everyone who works for them is thin, has straight white teeth, and are all-around heroes."[3]

As Baer's comments reveal, retirees are not bound by the Agency's criteria for assisting films, and for this precise reason the PAO is often concerned about their activities in Hollywood, especially since more and more are writing books based on their experiences.[4] Kent Harrington, a former CIA director of public affairs and two-time novelist, points out, "There are a lot of people who worked at CIA, and like an alumni of any organization, those people go off and do other things."[5] In recent decades, he explains, the Agency has relaxed the rules regarding what former officers can say and write about after their tenure with the Agency is over. This relaxation "has led to a mini-industry of people trying to sell stories to Hollywood or to write books that become movies."[6]

This "mini-industry" is particularly worrisome to the CIA's public relations team because, as Paul Barry explained, retired operatives are often "the last people we want representing the Agency . . . since many left disillusioned and pitch that perspective to Hollywood."[7] Harrington added that many retirees also pretend to have more knowledge about the Agency than they actually do. He cautions that Hollywood creators really have to look at retired personnel, "not as human beings, but in the sense of where did they come from, what part of the business were they in? How senior or junior were they? Were they in Washington or abroad? What can they be accurate about?"[8] In other words, he points out that an analyst who worked a desk job at the CIA and specialized in South American affairs would not be in a position to offer quality consultation on a film about field officers in Afghanistan, and creators should understand this distinction.

Harrington's point is a good one, since Hollywood often does not understand these distinctions, or, perhaps more simply, does not care about them. To cite just one example, Tony Mendez says that AMC asked him to appear on *Reel Talk* to discuss the historical accuracy of *Syriana*. But Mendez primarily worked in the CIA as a master of disguise in the Directorate of Science and Technology in the 1970s and 1980s; he was not an operations officer stationed in the Middle East, and thus it is not clear why he was the one asked to opine on the program. My guess is that AMC simply wanted an Agency representative to weigh in on the discussion and didn't care about Mendez's exact background, so long as they could display "former CIA officer" at the bottom of the screen when he appeared on the program.[9]

Baer and Bearden in Hollywood

Since the history of a retired CIA officer matters to an analysis of his or her films, a brief background on Baer and Bearden is in order, as is a description of the specific contributions each provided to *Syriana* and *The Good Shepherd*. Robert Baer served as a field officer for the CIA's Directorate of Operations from 1976 to 1997; for most of that time, he recruited and managed agents in the Middle East, working in Lebanon, Syria, Tajikistan, and Bosnia. Baer, who speaks Arabic, Farsi, Russian, and French, also served as the Iraqi bureau chief in the early to mid-1990s. His work won him the CIA's Career Intelligence Medal, and Seymour Hersh, the dean of intelligence reporters in Washington, DC, once acknowledged that Baer was viewed as "perhaps the best on-the-ground field officer in the Middle East."[10] Baer, however, came to an unhappy end at the CIA, as the Agency recalled him to Washington and accused him of plotting to kill Saddam Hussein.

As Christopher Ketcham explains, Baer was head of CIA operations in northern Iraq in 1995, where he was tasked with organizing opposition to Hussein. His sources inside the Iraqi army were plotting a coup, which Baer then worked to support. Washington would eventually claim that Baer had overstepped his authority in supporting the coup planners, although he claims that the Clinton administration had in fact given the go-ahead for the coup but then balked at the last minute. Thus he claims that he became the scapegoat for the White House's indecision and the quick failure of the coup when it finally unfolded.[11] In his memoir, Baer also asserts that Ahmed Chalabi, the head of an Iraqi dissident group, was the catalyst in his downward spiral within the Agency. According to Baer, Chalabi completely fabricated a story about a Robert Pope plotting to assassinate Hussein with the National Security Council's backing, and then fed the story to the Iranians in order to win their support for his party, which Chalabi argued would replace Hussein. When Tony Lake, Clinton's national security adviser, found out about the story, he was furious and recalled Baer to regain his turf in the Washington political scene by punishing the CIA.[12] Baer was eventually investigated by the FBI, had his passports confiscated, and was charged with attempted murder for conspiring to assassinate a foreign leader. After a six-month inquiry, he was exonerated of the charge but desk-jobbed at the CIA, which he quit shortly thereafter.[13]

Following his departure from the Agency, Baer published two memoirs: *See No Evil: The True Story of a Ground Soldier in the CIA's War on Terrorism* (2002) and *Sleeping with the Devil: How Washington Sold Our Soul for Saudi Crude* (2003). *See No Evil* recounts Baer's experiences working in the field and is critical of the Agency. He specifically lambastes the increasingly bureaucratic nature of the organization and its emphasis on political correctness rather than the tenacious elimination of security threats. He also chastises the CIA for its devaluation of human intelligence, its unwillingness to deal with unsavory types, and the way several Washington politicians, including Bill Clinton, compromise national security to please the big oil companies who contribute to their election campaigns.

Sleeping with the Devil addresses the politics of Saudi Arabia, a country ruled by a large and corrupt royal family that also controls much of the world's oil reserves. According to Baer, the Saudi royal family is one of the few groups able to stabilize oil prices by increasing production, but it is largely despised by its own citizens, who are growing increasingly fundamentalist in nature. In order to protect itself from a militant uprising, the Saudi rulers pay off militant Islamists (otherwise keen on their demise), including al-Qaeda. This arrangement means that the Saudis help fund Islamic militant causes in places like Afghanistan and terrorist action taken against the West. According to Baer, U.S. politicians have often ignored the corruption and danger presented by the Saudis because of the amount of money the royal family spends to influence powerful politicians and lobbyists, and because many politicians hope to engage in lucrative consulting jobs with the Saudis after their term is over.

Events presented in Baer's books served as the basis for the screenplay of the Academy Award–winning film *Syriana*, which starred George Clooney as Agent Bob Barnes, a loose version of Baer's life as a spy handler in the Middle East. Ultimately, the film considers the real price of oil and focuses on global petroleum politics as experienced by a CIA officer (Clooney), an energy analyst (Matt Damon), a young Pakistani migrant worker (Mazhar Munir) in an Arab country, a Washington attorney (Jeffrey Wright), and a host of Texan oil executives (Chris Cooper among them).

Undoubtedly, Baer's memoirs influenced the tone of Stephen Gaghan's screenplay, especially when it comes to its depiction of the CIA's treatment of Barnes. In *Syriana*, the CIA attempts to desk-job Barnes when he raises too many uncomfortable questions through his memos about arms trafficking in the Middle East. When the CIA realizes that Barnes lacks the political diplomacy needed for Washington, it again sends him into the field to assassinate Prince Nasir (a suspected terrorist), but when the plot threatens to become public, the CIA disowns Barnes. It paints him as a rogue agent, confiscates his passports, and orders an investigation, even though Barnes is one of the few officers with an intimate knowledge of the region and has recently been tortured, and nearly killed, while on assignment for the Agency. This story line has obvious parallels to Baer's own unhappy departure from the Agency, and certainly Baer's involvement with the film played a hand in its treatment of the CIA and Barnes.

But Baer did not just provide some of the source material for *Syriana*; he also introduced Gaghan to the world *Syriana* explored. The paired traveled around the Middle East and Europe for almost two months, attending oil conferences, meeting the spiritual head of Hezbollah, and cavorting with oil dealers in Nice.[14] Gaghan described Baer as his access point to "a total rogue's gallery—from government intelligence to middlemen in the oil business to arms dealers, terrorists, billionaires, and members of royal families from the oil-producing nations."[15] According to Gaghan, Baer also philosophized about the entire intelligence system, including the corruption in the FBI, the Justice Department, and the CIA, and claimed that he knew "every player in the oil business, every damn one."[16] As such, Gaghan claims that Baer actually proved a far better source of material than his memoirs, especially as he was willing to serve as Gaghan's guide to the "cultural and political machinations of the Middle East."[17]

Based on the above evidence, it is fair to classify Baer's involvement in *Syriana* as extensive, and because his involvement took place in the early stages of preproduction, he claims that the film is an accurate representation of its subject even though it is told through the conventions of a political thriller. Baer specifically argues that in most Hollywood films, technical consultation occurs just before a film enters into production. Such was the case in *Rendition*, when Baer was called in "at the last minute" to explain to the producers how cable traffic worked and what the CIA station in their mythical North African country might look like.[18] The producers, he explained, "were looking to increase the production values [of a few scenes] to add some sort of reality that would add to the drama." But the film itself is not realistic or authentic in terms of how rendition really works, he claims, primarily because no one who worked in intelligence was present in the film's research and writing stage. "If you compare their process to HBO's *The Wire*," he stated, "I think that it becomes clear that most Hollywood films have very little authenticity."[19] Baer's extensive and early association with *Syriana*, however, did help the film sell itself as an authentic, if highly fictionalized, docudrama—a pattern that repeated itself when Milt Bearden joined forces with the creators of *The Good Shepherd*.

Joining the Agency in 1964, Milt Bearden served as a station chief in Pakistan, Nigeria, Germany, and Sudan (and actually served as Baer's superior in Khartoum in the 1980s). During the same decade, Bearden also worked as a high-ranking officer in Afghanistan, where DCI William Casey deployed him to help fund and train the mujahedeen to fight the Soviet invasion, and later Bearden was appointed as the chief of the Soviet/East European Division during the collapse of the USSR. Throughout his thirty-year career, Bearden received several accolades, including the Distinguished Intelligence Medal, the Intelligence Medal of Merit, and the Donovan Award, and it seems that he left the Agency on friendly terms.

Following his retirement in 1994, Bearden began to write books and to try to sell his stories to Hollywood, joking that if he did not tell them, Oliver Stone would.[20] To date, those books include his cowritten memoir, *The Main Enemy: The Inside Story of the CIA's Final Showdown with the KGB* (2003), and a novel, *Black Tulip* (1998), set during the Russian occupation of Afghanistan. The screenwriter Eric Roth (*Munich* [2005], *The Good Shepherd*, *The Curious Case of Benjamin Button* [2008]) is reportedly working on an adaptation of *The Main Enemy*,[21] while Bearden's own film credits as technical consultant include *Meet the Parents*, *The Good Shepherd*, and *Charlie Wilson's War*.[22]

Of these three films, Bearden's influence is most significant in *The Good Shepherd*. While this film reached theaters in 2006, Bearden's work on the film actually began in the spring of 1997, when Robert De Niro discussed with Richard Holbrooke (former U.S. ambassador to the UN) his interest in directing a movie about the real world of American intelligence. Holbrooke wrote Bearden's phone number on the back of a cocktail napkin, since he had been the CIA chief when Holbrooke was ambassador to Germany in the early 1990s, and De Niro called him a few days later.[23]

Much like Baer, Bearden eventually developed a strong relationship with the film's director, taking De Niro around the world to meet members of the intelligence community. "Bob and I set off on a research journey that carried us to the Moscow underground," Bearden stated, "where De Niro spent a huge amount of time with my old adversaries in the KGB, watching them, and getting to understand them perhaps better than anyone other than someone who had spent a lifetime going against them in a Cold War struggle."[24] Bearden claims that this "De Niro research" produced the KGB character Ulysses in *The Good Shepherd*, and that later the pair traveled to Pakistan and Afghanistan "to get a feel for those theaters of struggle."[25]

The film's screenwriter, Eric Roth, also used Bearden's expertise and connections. Roth explained that he "constantly" used Bearden as a sounding board, asking him about how people in intelligence behave and how they might feel about certain things.[26] Bearden also introduced Roth and De Niro to a slew of intelligence officers over the years the film was in development. We once had "a big roundtable in Washington with 16 agents," Roth stated, before claiming that by the end of his research process, he had met with roughly forty CIA officers in total.[27] Additionally,

Bearden spent time explaining the intelligence world to the key actors, noting that De Niro involved him "in everything, from working with Eric on minor script issues, to casting, to set decoration, and props."[28]

Because of his extensive and early involvement, Bearden, like Baer, claims that "when the film was finally done . . . it was about as close to reality as we could get, bearing in mind that it was not intended as a documentary. The fact-based metaphor is the vehicle of this yarn," he stated, "and though some of the old hands of CIA might not have been as happy as I was with the end product, their problem was that they were looking for some sort of a recruiting film."[29] Indeed, the CIA was not pleased with *The Good Shepherd*. Paul Barry called the film a "lamentable piece of fiction masquerading as documentary,"[30] while CIA historians lambasted the film for "getting almost nothing right."[31]

Much of the CIA's disapproval regarding *The Good Shepherd* rests in its docudramatic qualities, as the film traces the evolution of the CIA from its days as the Office of Strategic Services to its involvement in the Bay of Pigs in the early 1960s, telling its story through composite characters based on actual CIA leaders. That both *The Good Shepherd* and *Syriana* were commercial successes starring high-profile actors only added to the CIA's woes. For instance, *Syriana* grossed $93.9 million in worldwide box office sales and an additional $15.8 million in the U.S. DVD market—not so bad for a film that cost only $50 million to make. Likewise, *Syriana*'s multiple, complicated, and intersecting story lines earned the film's writer-director an Academy Award nomination for Best Original Screenplay, while George Clooney won an Oscar for Best Supporting Actor in his role as Bob Barnes. *The Good Shepherd* fared even better at the box office, bringing in nearly $100 million in worldwide ticket sales and a $33.8 million domestic gross in DVD sales. The film also earned an Oscar nomination for Best Achievement in Art Direction in 2007.

Understanding the Agency's Disapproval of *Syriana* and *The Good Shepherd*

Perhaps because of these films' high profile, the CIA has publicly criticized *Syriana* and *The Good Shepherd* in interviews, lectures, and even scholarly publications.[32] These are all attempts to generate "flak," which Edward Herman and Noam Chomsky define as public statements by a group or individual trying to assail, threaten, or "correct" the media when it "[deviates] from the established line."[33] And it is easy to see why the CIA engaged in such actions. *Syriana* violates almost every criteria the CIA requires of scripts before it will offer assistance: it depicts the CIA in a negative light, it works to undermine employee morale, and it certainly fails to generate positive interest in the Agency. Clooney, after all, plays a character at the end of his career with no hopes for promotion. His family life is in shambles because of the constant traveling and secrecy his job demands (something that was more developed during production but cut in the editing stage). He is also tortured and nearly killed in the line of duty, but the Agency fails to reward his lifetime of service, and instead hangs him out to dry to protect its own interests.

The Agency itself is also depicted as failing to understand the seriousness and complexity of the Middle East and the geopolitics of oil. For instance, the CIA targets and assassinates Prince Nasir, a man suspected of selling weapons to militant groups intent on attacking the West. In reality, the British- and American-educated prince wants to gain control of his country in order to invest its oil profits in infrastructure, give rights to women, and build a democratic parliament as well as a middle class—thus the CIA ends up killing one of the region's best hopes for democracy. Early in the film, the CIA also ignores Barnes' memos that voice concerns about a missing weapon in the Middle East; according to the Agency, he "just doesn't get it; no one is interested in a missing weapon right now." That uninteresting weapon is used in a terrorist attack against a Western oil tanker at the end of the film, in a manner reminiscent of the 2000 attack on the USS *Cole* in Yemen.

The representations of the CIA in *The Good Shepherd* are not any better from the Agency's point of view. The film, in nonlinear fashion, traces the history of the CIA from the establishment of the OSS during World War II to its involvement in the Bay of Pigs in the 1960s, all through the character of Edward Wilson (Matt Damon). The film opens with a scene in which President Kennedy is heard stating that there will be no American intervention in Cuba, but shortly thereafter, the film cuts to Wilson in his office, where Richard Hayes tells him that it's "time to go to the beach." Bring your dancing shoes, too, he chides, since "we'll soon be doing the cha-cha." Of course, these opening scenes directly reference the Bay of Pigs and the CIA's false sense of confidence about the success of the operation, and its public attempts to mask its interference in Cuba.

The film goes on to focus on the CIA's more unsavory tactics. In one scene, Wilson asks a friend in the FBI for its files on DCI Phillip Allen, even though it is illegal for the CIA to spy on U.S. citizens. In yet another, the CIA tortures and waterboards a Soviet walk-in, and when that fails to produce the "evidence" they seek, they administer LSD as a truth serum, which only succeeds at causing the Russian to commit suicide while high. (Viewers later learn that the Russian would have been an actual asset to the United States, able to unmask a double agent working within the CIA.) Perhaps the most egregious action, however, occurs after Wilson's son joins the CIA and falls in love with a Soviet officer while stationed in the Congo. Ulysses, the chief of Russian counterintelligence, tells Wilson that the woman has truly fallen in love with his son, but neither of them can ever be sure of her allegiance. Thus Wilson arranges for his future daughter-in-law's death, having her pushed out of an airplane on the way to her wedding. Wilson later learns that the woman was pregnant and thus he has killed not only his son's fiancée, but also his own grandchild, all in the name of national security. Paul Barry states that these types of scenes "not only disparage the reputations of our officers but negatively influence the decisions of potential assets contemplating an association with the CIA."[34] This point is well-taken, but it is important to add that the CIA's disapproval of both *The Good Shepherd* and *Syriana* was not founded just on a basic textual analysis of the films. It was also compounded by the films' associations with retired CIA officers and their docudramatic elements, which both suggested to viewers that the films were plausible and even historically accurate.

The Special Problem of the Docudrama

Basically defined, the docudrama is a film that "blends fact and fiction to dramatize events and historic personages,"[35] although it runs across a spectrum that ranges from "journalistic reconstruction to relevant drama with infinite graduations along the way."[36] While *Syriana* is more fictionalized than *The Good Shepherd*, it nonetheless fits the description of a docudrama since it was based on Baer's real-life experiences, the specific character Robert Barnes is based on Baer, and the film used composites of real people to form its supporting cast.[37] Further, viewers understood the film as a docudrama because its director of photography, Robert Elswit, tackled *Syriana* with a quasi-documentary strategy, relying on two hand-held cameras for shooting and attempting to capture what each location would look like in natural light.[38]

For each of these reasons, the public discourse surrounding *Syriana*'s release focused on notions of historical accuracy. For instance, in an interview with Baer for the *New Republic*, Devin Faraci began by asking exactly how "real" the film was.[39] Baer responded that the "movie is absolutely authentic," adding that he doesn't usually watch movies, and would never watch a spy movie, but that *Syriana* was "based on everybody I knew in this world."[40] The interview then launched into specific elements of the film's authenticity, as Baer explained that in the film the CIA uses bad information to target and ultimately assassinate Prince Nasir. The former operative explained that the CIA does engage in these types of "lethal findings," despite Executive Order 12333, which prohibits any U.S. government employee from engaging in assassination. He offered the case of Muammar Gaddafi as evidence, and a recent event in Yemen where the CIA fired a missile into a car carrying six people, killing all of them. "They're trying to kill bin Laden with Predators [too]," he added. "It does happen."

In an interview for National Public Radio, Robert Siegel likewise questioned Baer about the plausibility of the film, asking about a scene where a former CIA contractor discusses the abduction of Nasir from an oil-producing state in the Middle East. "Plausible—such things have really happened, or a good fiction writer's conceit?"[41] Baer answers assuredly: "It's more than plausible." He then explains that in 1997, he left the Agency and travelled to Beirut, where there was a contract out on a Gulf prince. The prince opposed his government and had even led an attempted coup in 1995. He was trying the coup again in 1997, he said, so "there was money being offered to whack this guy. . . . This is the way the Middle East works." When Siegel then asked about the scene where Barnes is tortured, Baer noted that CIA officers have occasionally been tortured, including the Beirut station chief Bill Buckley, who was kidnapped in Lebanon in the spring of 1984 and tortured to death by the summer of 1985, likely by members of Hezbollah.

This discourse, which painted *Syriana* as an accurate depiction of the CIA's work, angered the Agency, which is actively trying to reverse its image as a trigger-happy, incompetent outfit. And precisely because of the film's connection to Baer, those in the CIA often dismissed *Syriana* as little more than the product of a disillusioned operative looking to settle an old score. For instance, the CIA general counsel John Rizzo characterized Baer as an officer who "left the Agency rather embittered. It's unfortunate but it does happen; more unfortunate is that officers of this kind write books. But you get this; you get disgruntled people. He was a talented officer, and for all I know, he was not used well. But CIA is like any other profession; you get screwed sometimes."[42] (Rizzo, however, never mentions Baer's recall, and thus ignores the fact that Baer, unlike most professionals, risked his life abroad only to be tried by his own government for attempted murder.) Tony Mendez, less drastically, called *Syriana* "a real downer for the Agency," and suggested that it was a product of an officer who had had "a relatively short career" within the Agency before leaving disillusioned[43]—even though Baer worked for the Agency for more than twenty years.

As if anticipating these types of criticisms, the special features section of *Syriana*'s DVD presents Clooney describing Baer as someone who was "a true believer" and "not a cynic." Clooney argues that Baer truly believed that working for the Agency was "the right thing to do to help his country," before explaining that Baer became disillusioned with the CIA because, ultimately, "the Company let him down." Clooney claims that Baer was part of the "downsizing that happened to everyone at the CIA" at the end of the Cold War; but, of course, Baer was not exactly downsized, and Clooney's comments erase the more controversial politics surrounding Baer's recall to Washington and the subsequent investigation about his role in the Iraqi coup.

These competing versions of Baer reflect the fact that history is never spelled with a capital *H*, and that the history of any person, place, or film comprises multiple perspectives. But *Syriana* also highlights the fact that filmmakers are historians, too, documenting, in a public medium, their version of events, which may ultimately hold more sway over the public's understanding than any "sober historian mired in tons of data" might accomplish.[44] And it is this power of filmmaking that gives the CIA pause, because, even by the CIA's own admission, films such as *Syriana* are much more influential in shaping the public's understanding of the Agency than any news article, memo, or report that it may release—especially when viewers understand that the film is based, to some degree, on actual figures and events.

As such, the docudramatic elements of *The Good Shepherd* proved even more disturbing to the CIA than those in *Syriana*, since almost all its characters are composites of well-known figures in the intelligence community, and the film directly references real-world events through the use of actual news footage. For instance, the character Arch Cummings is largely based on Kim Philby, the famous Cambridge spy who worked for the Russians while serving Britain's MI6 for more than thirty years before defecting to the Soviet Union. Likewise, De Niro's character, General Bill Sullivan, is loosely based on General "Wild Bill" Donovan, the head of the OSS during World War II, while Richard Hayes is loosely based on Richard Helms, DCI from 1966 to 1973. Even Wilson's character is partially based on James Jesus Angleton, the founder of CIA counterintelligence, while Phillip Allen was modeled after DCI Allen Dulles.

Because of these historical links, *The Good Shepherd* pitched itself as "the true story of the birth of the CIA" and "the untold story of the most powerful covert agency in the world." Eric Roth also touted the film as the most realistic picture ever made about the CIA, while Gary Crowdus of *Cineaste* claims that *The Good Shepherd* is "without question one of the most realistic films ever made about the actual craft of intelligence."[45] Even the film's website helped to market the text as historical, since it provided "further reading lists" and educational guides, much in the way that documentaries might.[46] These claims of history and truthfulness infuriated the CIA to the point that one of its historians likened the film to a "sin" because it says "it's the truth when it's not, and they know it's not."[47]

Perhaps more interesting, however, is the fact that after the film's release, a team of Agency historians actually set out to discredit the film's claims to historical accuracy through its journal, *Studies in Intelligence*, and Nicholas Dujmovic furthered those in an article in *Intelligence and National Security*. Since many of the ideas presented in Dujmovic's article are present in the joint piece, I will focus on the joint article, which appeared in the "Intelligence in Public Media" section and features the opinions of three historians working at the CIA's Center for the Study of Intelligence.

The piece begins by arguing that the film's taglines failed to present the film as a transparent fiction, and that by using composite characters modeled on real CIA officers, placing them in scenarios based on historical events, and paying careful attention to sets and costumes, *The Good Shepherd* communicates a strong degree of authenticity reminiscent of Oliver Stone's *JFK* (1991). Yet such storytelling devices, they argue, conflate fact and fiction, potentially leading viewers to believe that the film is an authentic and historically accurate retelling of the CIA's early history. In order to dispel this notion, the piece outlines many of the historical inaccuracies in the film (see table 6.1 for a taste). These include the idea that the Bay of Pigs operation failed because someone leaked the name of the landing site, but as history shows, "there were plenty of problems with the Bay of Pigs on the policy side, on the planning side, and on the execution side," and no one has ever blamed the disaster on a single leak.[48] Additionally, the film's DCI, Philip Allen, is forced to resign after the Bay of Pigs for tucking money away in a Swiss bank account. Allen's character is based on DCI Allen Dulles, who was forced to resign in 1961 after the Bay of Pigs fiasco but primarily because Kennedy needed a public gesture of accountability for the failed operation. The authors also lament the fact that

Table 6.1. *The Good Shepherd*'s CIA and the Historical Reality

Character (Actor)	Real-life Model
Edward Wilson (Matt Damon): Inducted into Yale's Skull and Bones society and is mentored by its members in CIA.	**James Angleton**: Went to Yale but was not a member of Skull and Bones.

Comment: Wilson is primarily patterned after Angleton but he could be Frank Wisner (University of Virginia), William Harvey (Indiana), Richard Bissel or Tracy Barnes (Yale, but not Skull and Bones).

Character (Actor)	Real-life Model
Philip Allen (William Hurt): A Skull and Bones hierarch.	**Allen Dulles**: A Princeton graduate.

Comment: The character who is Wilson's wife (Angelina Jolie) is named "Clover," the name of Allen Dulles's wife. Philip Allen's wife is called "Blossom."

Character (Actor)	Real-life Model
Richard Hayes (Lee Pace): A Skull and Bones brother.	**Richard Helms**: Went to Williams College.

Comment: Hayes succeeds Allen as CIA director in the film, skipping over Dulles's real successor, John McCone (UC Berkeley).

Character (Actor)	Real-life Model
William Sullivan (Robert De Niro)	**William Donovan**

Comment: Playing the founder of OSS, De Niro alternatively is preachy, moralistic, and cynical. Donovan was none of these.

Character (Actor)	Real-life Model
Ray Brocco (John Turturro)	**Ray Rocca**

Comment: Rocca was Angleton's loyal deputy for years—as an analyst, not an operations officer.

Character (Actor)	Real-life Model
Sam Murach (Alec Baldwin)	**Sam Papich**

Comment: FBI agent Papich was the long-time go-between for J. Edgar Hoover and CIA, especially to the CI staff.

Character (Actor)	Real-life Model
Yuri Modin, the false Valentin Mironov (John Sessions)	**Anatoliy Golitsyn**

Comment: Golitsyn was the first of two Soviet defectors. Angleton trusted him; beyond that, the film depiction bears no relationship to reality.

Character (Actor)	Real-life Model
Valentin Mironov (Mark Ivanir)	**Yuri Nosenko**

Comment: The interrogation of Mironov, with its use of violence and drugs, bears no resemblance to Nosenko's actual treatment.

Character (Actor)	Real-life Model
Arch Cummings (Billy Crudup)	**Harold "Kim" Philby**

Comment: Philby was sidelined from intelligence long before the Golitsyn/Nosenko matter, but in the film, Modin is Cummings's agent.

Character (Actor)	Real-life Model
Stas Siyanko/"Ulysses" (Oleg Stefan)	**None**

Comment: The only "human" character in the film has no real-life counterpart.

Source: David Robarge, Gary McCollim, Nicholas Dujmovic, and Thomas G. Coffey, "Intelligence in Public Media: *The Good Shepherd*," *Studies in Intelligence* 50, no. 1 (2007): 47–54.

the film omits all of the CIA's successes of the time (including the Berlin Tunnel), which suggests to viewers that during the early years of the CIA, the Agency failed to do anything of long-term strategic importance.

As Robert Rosenstone argues, these types of complaints are commonly launched at docudramas, which are criticized for bending history, willfully mixing fact and fiction, failing to delineate between evidence and speculation, and creating characters that never existed and incidents that never occurred.[49] These complaints, he explains, are based on the notion that a historical film is no more than a piece of written history transferred to the screen and that history is little more than a compilation of undisputable facts.[50] Such notions, however, fail to recognize the basic demands of Hollywood films, which must use invention to fit the demands of dramatic structure. Rosenstone argues this point by explaining that in *JFK*, Oliver Stone invents Donald Sutherland's Deep Throat–type character to help Jim Garrison (Kevin Costner) make sense of all the evidence he has gathered; according to Rosenstone, Oliver Stone is doing no more than finding a plausible, dramatic way of summarizing "evidence that comes from too many sources to depict on the screen."[51] For similar reasons, the Hollywood historical film also includes images that are at once invented but may still be considered true—"true in that they symbolize, condense or summarize larger amounts of data," or "true in that they carry out the overall meaning of the past that can be documented or verified."[52]

The real merit of a docudrama, Rosenstone insists, does not rest in how much period detail or flat facts a film disseminates. Rather, its merits rest in the ways it serves to provoke thought about larger historical issues. So, just as *JFK* asked if something has gone wrong with the United States since the 1960s, *The Good Shepherd* and *Syriana* ask if something has gone wrong with the CIA post-9/11, or if anything about the Agency was ever right. Given that both these films debuted when the CIA was being harshly criticized for failing to predict 9/11, misunderstanding the presence of WMDs in Iraq, engaging in waterboarding and extraordinary rendition, and running private interrogation camps abroad, the films asked viewers to analyze the present state of the CIA through the prism of the past, fulfilling what Rosenstone calls the docudrama's burden of asking viewers to "rethink how we got where we are and to make us question the values that we and our leaders and our nation live by."[53]

Rosenstone's ideas have made a significant impact on scholars' understanding of the role of docudrama, but other critics are not as willing to dismiss the responsibilities of any form that claims to be historically accurate. In fact, because docudramas signify a contract between the creators and the audience, which suggests that the text is based, to some degree, on historical facts, the documentary filmmaker Leslie Woodhead writes that makers of docudramas have a special obligation to not deliberately mislead the audience; in fact, he calls for creators to signpost material to avoid "as far as possible a confusion in the audience about levels of credibility."[54] The filmmaker and scholar Alan Rosenthal takes more of a middle ground, explaining that while viewers understand that docudramas blend fact and fiction and take artistic license, there are obvious situations where the "mixing of fact with fiction and dramatizations masquerading as documentary are misleading."[55] These situations arise when the audience completely, or almost completely, misreads the fiction as fact, and when the misleading fictional elements are of real consequence to the story or to the sense of the characters. Additionally, he writes, concerns arise when the subject being presented is "one that can, or is meant to, affect our ongoing social or political actions and attitudes in a fairly important way."[56]

Given Rosenthal's second and third points, it is easy to see why the CIA has felt the need to generate flak regarding films like *The Good Shepherd*, since the license it takes in depicting CIA leadership as morally bankrupt is central to viewers' understanding of the characters, and by extension, the Agency. Additionally, the film's fictionalized ending presents serious concerns for the CIA. Earlier in the film, Bill Sullivan fears that in creating a central intelligence agency, "too much power will end up in the hands of too few." "It's always in somebody's best interest," he states, "to promote enemies real or imagined. I want this to be the eyes and ears of America — not its heart and soul." That is why, the film explains, he demands civilian oversight of the Agency's actions. But these lines are nearly reversed at the end of the film when Wilson is walking with the Agency's new DCI, Richard Hayes. Examining its new headquarters, Hayes tells Wilson to look around while he attends an oversight meeting. "Can you imagine?" Hayes scoffs. "They think they can look into our closet. As if we'd let them." Hayes then turns to Wilson before adding, "I remember a senator once asked me, when we talk about CIA why we never use the word 'the' in front of it. And I asked him, do you put the word 'the' in front of God?"

This ending suggests that the CIA, within a short span of time, had gone from a well-intentioned, democratic institution to one filled with corrupt and arrogant megalomaniacs. Given the time of the film's release (discussed above), it is clear that the filmmakers were trying to affect viewers' "ongoing social or political actions and attitudes in a fairly important way" by suggesting that the CIA has almost always been corrupt, paranoid, and untrustworthy. Anyone other than a CIA expert viewing the film is likely to be, in the words of Rosenstone, "confronted with a linear story that is unproblematic and uncontested in its view of what happened and why."[57]

The CIA, recognizing this element, has thus grown concerned over its image in the docudrama, and the way that the genre's recent attachment to retired CIA operatives lends greater authenticity to the productions. Even Dujmovic admits that he was initially excited about *The Good Shepherd*'s release because he had heard that the film was eight years in the making and used a former officer as its consultant, which led him to believe the film would indeed be historically accurate.[58]

But even though the CIA Public Affairs Office claims that the retired officer is often the last person it wants representing the Agency in Hollywood, this does not mean that the Agency is always disserved by the docudrama or the retiree. A good case in point is *Charlie Wilson's War*, a docudrama on which Milt Bearden served as a technical consultant, significantly assisting the director, Mike Nichols, during the production stages. This film centers around Charlie Wilson (Tom Hanks), a womanizing Texas congressman who sits on two major foreign policy and covert operations committees. Through his relationship with Joanne Herring (Julia Roberts) and the maverick CIA agent Gust Avrakotos (Philip Seymour Hoffman), Wilson sets out to defeat the Soviets in Afghanistan, and together, the team is able to supply the Afghan mujahedeen with the weapons and support they need to successfully defeat the Red Army.

Admittedly, the film is mixed in its representations of the CIA, as its station chiefs and upper management are depicted as ineffectual at best, but the film's main CIA representative, Gust, is an intelligent, competent, and likeable officer. He is able to devise a strategy for defeating the Soviets and understands, more than the U.S. Congress, the need for Americans to assist in the rebuilding of Afghanistan, lest the Soviet withdrawal creates a power vacuum and "the crazies" start "rolling into Kandahar." As Baer explains, "I don't think [*Charlie Wilson's War*] was anti-CIA at all," and even Barry praised the film as a generally "positive portrayal of a CIA accomplishment."[59]

Additionally, when I asked Baer to comment on Paul Barry's assertion that retired CIA operatives are often the last people he wants representing the Agency in Hollywood (because they often pitch a disillusioned view), Baer quipped, "Well, I would say that if a CIA retiree does leave disillusioned then what does that say [about the CIA]?" He then continued, more seriously, "Look, it's not like Hollywood goes around asking people, are you disillusioned with the CIA, and if they say yes, only then will they say, great, we want to talk to you. Hollywood finds whom it can find. It's mostly looking for a good story line, so if any retired CIA operative has one, regardless of their opinions of the Agency, I think Hollywood is interested." That Bearden worked on both *The Good Shepherd* and *Charlie Wilson's War* gives weight to this claim, and suggests that the CIA places too much emphasis on the idea that many retirees leave the Agency disillusioned or that they have the power to sell their perspective to Hollywood wholesale.

In fact, the role of the retired CIA officer in Hollywood is an incredibly important one. Yes, there certainly are members of the CIA who experienced strong disillusionment who now work in Hollywood, and yes, there are several other ex-CIA members interested in honoring the work they engaged in for so long. Both camps have an important perspective to share with the Hollywood community and, by extension, the viewing public, because when viewed in total, this body of work has the best chance of painting a knowledgeable, accurate, and balanced portrayal of the Agency for viewers—something the CIA's Public Affairs Office will never do.

Conclusion

Since the CIA first started appearing in motion pictures in the 1960s, the Agency has been depicted in a very negative light. Indeed, Hollywood's most common constructions of Langley revolved around the image of the CIA as a rogue organization, working outside effective oversight; as a malicious organization that betrays its own assets and officers; as possessing a strong predilection toward assassination; or as a buffoonish and hopelessly inept outfit. Given this cinematic history, it is understandable that the CIA wished to reverse its popular image by working with motion picture creators, but given its culture of secrecy, it did not actually embark on the public mission until the 1990s.

During the early part of the 1990s, the CIA experienced a number of setbacks that finally demanded that it become more proactive in shaping its image at home. These challenges included the collapse of the Soviet Union, which left many to question whether the CIA was still needed in a post–Cold War era, and the highly publicized case of Aldrich Ames, who not only highlighted the CIA's failure to weed out a mole in operation for nearly a decade, but who also publicly claimed that the intelligence business was a "sham" since the information the Agency collected was rarely valuable to policy makers' needs. Accusations that government agencies had grown too secretive—and thus prohibited citizens from gaining the information they needed to valuably participate in a democracy—also played a role in the CIA's public affairs crisis during the 1990s.

Collectively, these issues pushed the CIA into a collaboration with film and television producers, in order to shape its domestic image and reassure citizens and Congress that the Agency was still necessary and valuable. This agenda started with the tightly controlled television series project called *The Classified Files of the CIA*, but after that failed to air, the

Agency began trying subtler and more informal approaches to dealing with Hollywood.

Most of these efforts are initiated by the CIA's entertainment liaison or media relations team. Because these officials lack access to the expensive equipment the Pentagon leverages to influence script changes as a project nears production, however, the Agency is better suited to influencing texts during the preproduction stages, when the images of the Agency are first being crafted. To achieve this goal, the Agency's Public Affairs Office works to provide creators with advice, technical consultation, and access to its campus and officers in order to help shape the Agency's image. On rarer occasions, the CIA has even hosted a project's premiere at a red-carpet event to which prominent members of the press, intelligence, and entertainment communities are invited. But the CIA will provide these services *only* for projects whose scripts it has reviewed in advance and which depict the Agency in a favorable light. Creators of works that the CIA believes will not generate a favorable image of Langley, aid in its recruitment efforts, increase understanding of the Agency, or instill pride in its employees, are either asked to alter their depictions of the CIA or simply denied government assistance.

This process of exerting government influence on Hollywood texts is not a heavy-handed approach to creating propaganda. Television and film creators are always free to refuse the CIA's demanded changes and are not at the mercy of formal CIA censorship. Nonetheless, the relationship between the CIA and Hollywood is troublesome for numerous reasons. For one, creators who are looking to enhance the authenticity of their texts by conducting research through CIA resources, or who are simply looking to film on the Agency's premises, understand that in order to receive these services they must depict the Agency sympathetically. Thus a type of self-censorship, motivated by financial and creative gains (rather than sheer ideological ones), plays a role in the shaping of motion picture content. Likewise, those seeking initial CIA consultation and advice are often treated to a whitewashed version of the Agency, where valid criticisms are downplayed or even ignored. This is partially evidenced by the entertainment liaison's webpage, where the CIA offers up a host of possible story lines for screenwriters to explore, all of which are examples of CIA successes. But this is not surprising, given that the Office of Public Affairs, whose very job is to represent the Agency in a positive light, handles the large majority of entertainment requests.

Additionally, I contend, by refusing to offer its assistance and resources to filmmakers whose depiction of the CIA it does not like, the CIA, like many other government agencies, is in violation of the First Amendment. Not all scholars agree with this assertion. For instance, when speaking about the Pentagon's relationship with Hollywood, the military historian Lawrence Suid argues that the idea, "[that] filmmakers should have access to military men and equipment whether or not a service likes a particular script" is absurd.[1] "By that logic," he writes,

> any citizen could knock on the door of Air Force One and demand to be taken to his or her destination since the citizen paid taxes. Yes, the armed services require that a production must offer benefit to them or be in their best interest to qualify for assistance. General Motors was never going to help Ralph Nader make a movie about the Corvair. No organization wants to be portrayed negatively. Why should the armed services be any different and be required to provide help to a film which portrays historical events or military procedures inaccurately?[2]

Likewise, Paul Barry likened the CIA's decision on whether it should assist scripts to corporate sponsorship decisions, since the Agency wants to support only those projects that will project the right brand image.[3]

The problem with both Barry's and Suid's comments, however, is that private corporations are not bound to the First Amendment in the same way as the government. After all, the First Amendment states that *Congress* shall make no law "abridging the freedom of speech, or of the press." Over time, this amendment has been more broadly interpreted to mean that the government is not allowed to use its resources to discriminate against some citizens and favor others based on their viewpoint or perspective. Private corporations are free to do this; government agencies are not. Also, government agencies do not simply reject filmmakers because the films in question depict the government inaccurately; they also reject filmmakers because those works project the government in a negative light or fail to aid in recruitment or boost internal morale. The concept of accuracy is just one of many considerations the government uses to assess the value of assisting a particular project. Additionally, the government's efforts also violate the spirit, and perhaps even the letter, of the publicity and propaganda laws, which prevent the government from engaging in self-aggrandizement, puffery, and covert communication.

Indeed, the CIA's relationship with Hollywood would perhaps be less objectionable if it were clearer to viewers that the Agency is involved in the shaping of its content. But in television series, Agency officers are almost never credited, either in the episode credits or on the Internet Movie

Database. In films, the CIA or one of its technical consultants are some-times credited and even featured in a DVD segment, but even here, the credits appear in small font at the very end of the film or are not totally accurate about the position of the person being highlighted. Likewise, while the Pentagon and the FBI have made their files available to the pub-lic, either through Freedom of Information Act requests or through dona-tions to university libraries, the CIA has yet to release more than a hand-ful of files documenting its relationship with Hollywood. Those that have been released are mostly internal newsletter stories or press releases that celebrate a premiere or an actor's visit to the campus, and none documents the changes the CIA has demanded of a particular project.

Despite these ethical and legal concerns, the CIA has been subtlety in-fluencing motion picture content for more than fifteen years now. When one looks at the list of films and series that the Agency has assisted — including *The Recruit, The Sum of All Fears, The Agency, In the Company of Spies, Covert Affairs,* and others — it becomes clear that the old, negative images of the Agency have been reversed. Instead of featuring an inept organization full of conspiratorial assassins, these texts depict a morally upright organization that effectively thwarts national security threats and presents its employees with challenging and rewarding work. These works also encourage viewers to curtail their criticisms of the Agency by consid-ering the fact that when the CIA is successful in neutralizing a threat, no one ever hears about it. When the CIA fails, however, the press widely cir-culates the story, so, the Agency argues, the public gets a distorted view of the outfit's effectiveness.

Perhaps even more important, all these texts sidestep important issues surrounding the CIA, especially those films and series released since 9/11. For instance, in recent years, the CIA has come under fire for engaging in rendition and torture, running secret interrogation camps abroad, and de-stroying interrogation tapes. It has also faced criticism for lacking enough officers with relevant language skills, for lacking valuable human assets in Afghanistan, Iraq, and Pakistan who can provide the Agency with valu-able intelligence, and for outsourcing much of its intelligence work to private companies like Blackwater/Xe. Explorations of these criticisms are not present in any CIA-related text, except to suggest that the CIA has already corrected the problem (and thus the issue is not really a problem). Likewise, films that have featured these issues, such as the CIA torturing or waterboarding suspects, have been explicitly denied Agency assistance.

I am not trying to argue that the old images of the CIA are any more realistic than the images that now appear in CIA-assisted texts — neither are an accurate, or even balanced, portrayal of the Agency. What I am trying to point out is that the CIA is trying to circulate whitewashed images of itself through popular media. Further, it is trying to weave those images into the fabric of society in such a way that viewers see them as a "natural" reflection of the Agency, rather than one that is partially constructed and manipulated by the government.

Interestingly, this issue may soon have relevance beyond the domestic scene. More specifically, the CIA is now poised to expand its liaison relationships to foreign markets. In 2010, the CIA Public Affairs officer Paula Weiss stated that the CIA regularly receives between forty to sixty requests from both domestic and foreign filmmakers each month.[4] These requests range from the acquisition of photographs of the compound, to stock footage, to technical consultation, to meetings with the D/CIA and other Agency officers. In the past, Barry stated, the CIA had not worked extensively with foreign filmmakers, since non-U.S. citizens are not allowed onto the CIA's campus and thus the liaison officer could not offer many services.[5] Now, Weiss explains, the CIA's media relations team is able to assist these filmmakers remotely through videoconferencing technology.[6]

Barry admitted that he found the opportunity to influence foreign audiences intriguing, and argued that the burgeoning film industry in the Middle East might provide a huge opportunity for the CIA in the future, presumably because it could help make the Agency appear more favorably and encourage potential assets in the region to volunteer their services. It will be interesting to see how and if the image of the CIA changes in foreign films in the future, and what sort of ramifications this may have for the international community.

Notes

Introduction

1. Alford and Graham, "Lights, Camera."
2. Aldrich, "Regulation by Revelation?," 17–18.
3. Paul Barry quoted in Jenkins, "How the Central Intelligence Agency Works with Hollywood," 490–491. According to Barry, Chase Brandon took his contacts and files in order to build his own Hollywood consulting business in the private sector.
4. Alford and Graham, "Lights, Camera."
5. Central Intelligence Agency, "About CIA."
6. Kessler, *Inside the CIA*, 1.
7. Ibid., 3.
8. Central Intelligence Agency, "Support to Mission."
9. The Department of Defense, by comparison, has a much larger staff. According to Jeff Clark, who handles public inquires for the Assistant Secretary of Defense, his public affairs office houses 123 employees, with 93 who serve as public affairs professionals (as opposed to administrative support and IT workers). This number does not include those employees who serve in the DOD's armed services branches, including the army, navy, and air force, each of which has its own public affairs teams. Jeff Clark, phone interview with the author, March 17, 2010.
10. Wilford, *Mighty Wurlitzer*, 117.
11. Eldridge, "Dear Owen," 154.
12. Ibid., 155.
13. Ibid., 159.
14. Alford and Graham, "Lights, Camera."
15. The OPC operated under the direction of the Departments of State and Defense but was housed at the CIA, where it received administrative support and was eventually absorbed in 1951. Shaw, *Hollywood's Cold War*, 75–79.
16. Ibid., 75.
17. Ibid., 76.
18. Ibid., 77.

19. The last few sentences of Orwell's novel read, "Twelve voices were shouting in anger, and they were all alike. No question, now, what had happened to the faces of the pigs. The creatures outside looked from pig to man, and from man to pig, and from pig to man again; but already it was impossible to say which was which." Orwell's ending clearly indicts both the governments of capitalists (the men) and communists (the pigs), suggesting that there is little difference in their overall effect on the human condition and that absolute power corrupts absolutely. The film version, however, virtually removes the capitalist farmers from the final scene and works to incite an uprising against communist leadership.

20. Leab, *Orwell Subverted*, 137.

21. Shaw, *Hollywood's Cold War*, 108.

22. Gribble, "Anti-communism, Patrick Peyton, CSC, and the CIA," 543.

23. Ibid., 545.

24. Leab, *Orwell Subverted*, 93.

25. Ibid.

26. Bushnell, "Paying for the Damage," 38.

27. Ibid., 39.

28. Rositzke, *CIA's Secret Operations*, 156.

29. The "Mighty Wurlitzer" is a term applied by the CIA to its cultural propaganda campaign during the Cold War. This program often used entertainment stars to promote capitalism throughout Eastern Europe and South Asia.

30. Tony Mendez, personal interview with the author, March 5, 2008.

31. Paul Barry, personal interview with the author, March 4, 2008.

32. Chambers is called "Jerome Calloway" in Mendez's book *Master of Disguise*, so as not to violate CIA regulations about the disclosure of assets.

33. Mendez, *Master of Disguise*, 119.

34. Ibid.

35. Ibid., 276.

36. According to Tony Mendez, the CIA is not allowed to use the media, religious groups, students, or the Peace Corps as a cover unless it has director approval, thus explaining why film-crew covers were unusual for the CIA to employ.

37. Mendez, personal interview with the author.

38. Ibid.

Chapter 1

1. Bernstein, "Hardest-Working Actor of the Season."

2. Ibid.

3. Williams, "Chase Brandon."

4. Argetsinger and Roberts, "CIA Has a New Man on a Special Mission."

5. Lundegaard, "You're Not Reading This."

6. Ibid.

7. Bill Harlow quoted in Loeb, "CIA's Operation Hollywood."

8. Chase Brandon quoted in Robb, *Operation Hollywood*, 149.

9. Sailer, "*The Recruit*."

10. For instance, during my interview with the CIA historian Nicholas Duj-

movie on March 15, 2009, he claimed that "there is no historical basis" for any of the five representations that I highlight in this chapter.

11. See, for instance, Bill Harlow in Loeb, "CIA's Operation Hollywood," and Paul Barry in Jenkins, "How the Central Intelligence Agency Works with Hollywood," 493.

12. "Executive Order 12333—United States Intelligence Activities."

13. See, for instance, Lumpkin, "U.S. Can Target American al-Qaida Agents."

14. Doyle and Kornbluh, "CIA and Assassinations."

15. The Church Committee reports can be viewed at the Assassination Archives and Research Center website at http://www.aarclibrary.org/publib/contents/church/contents_church_reports.htm.

16. Miller, "CIA-Blackwater Assassination Contract Points to Larger Connections"; Flintoff, "How Far Did CIA Assassination Plans Go?"

17. Hersh, "Huge CIA Operation Reported in U.S. against Anti-war Forces."

18. For more information, see Weiner, *Legacy of Ashes*.

19. James Grady, e-mail to the author, March 15, 2010.

20. McGilligan, *"Three Days of the Condor."*

21. Dujmovic, "Two CIA Prisoners in China."

22. Dujmovic, personal interview with the author.

23. More specifically, Watergate involved five "former" CIA operatives breaking into the Democratic National Committee headquarters on behalf of President Nixon to help his reelection campaign, while the Iran-Contra scandal featured the CIA working to facilitate the sale of arms to Iran—the subject of an arms embargo—in order to secure the release of American hostages taken by Hezbollah and fund Nicaraguan contras.

24. Armando Spataro quoted in De Cristofaro and Rotella, "Italy Judge Convicts 23 Americans in 2003 CIA Kidnapping of Egyptian Cleric."

25. Douglas, *"Rendition* Writer Kelley Sane."

26. Mel Brooks quoted in Green, *"Get Smart" Handbook*, 9.

27. Gary McCollim quoted in Robarge, "Intelligence in Recent Public Media."

28. The Bay of Pigs operation involved training a group of Cuban exiles to launch a military attack against Fidel Castro in 1961. The invaders were disguised as Cuban defectors to hide U.S. involvement in the plot, and the CIA had counted on local support for the uprising against Castro to assist in the offensive. The operation, however, proved an utter failure, as CIA leadership failed to understand that many Cubans supported Castro and the revolution and thus local support never arrived. The invasion itself was also poorly executed by DCI Allen Dulles and CIA officer Richard Bissell, both of whom were fired by President Kennedy shortly thereafter.

29. The Agency was reportedly trying to take out the headquarters of the Yugoslav Federal Directorate for Supply and Procurement.

30. The Bond specialist John Cork quoted in Vinciguerra, "Holmes Had Watson."

31. Ibid.

32. Ibid.

33. This statement was remembered by Bill Harlow in a personal interview with the author on January 22, 2010.

34. Ibid.

35. Ibid.

36. American Civil Liberties Union, "Celebrities Speak Out for Civil Liberties in New ACLU Advertising Campaign."

37. Ibid.

38. Doyle, "End of Secrecy," 35.

39. Ibid.

40. Ibid.

41. Grady, e-mail to the author. Grady contacted the CIA several times while reporting for the syndicated columnist Jack Anderson.

42. Dujmovic, personal interview with the author.

43. Chase Brandon quoted in Robb, *Operation Hollywood*, 151.

44. Grady, e-mail to the author.

45. Peter Iliff, e-mail to the author, March 28, 2010.

Chapter 2

Portions of this chapter previously appeared in "Get Smart: A Look at the Current Relationship between Hollywood and the CIA," *Historical Journal of Film, Radio, and Television* 29, no. 2 (June 2009): 229–243. These portions are reprinted here with permission.

1. Paul Barry quoted in Jenkins, "How the Central Intelligence Agency works with Hollywood," 490.

2. Ibid.

3. Chase Brandon quoted in Paramount Pictures, *"The Sum of All Fears."*

4. Bolten, "Enforcing the CIA's Secrecy Agreement," 409.

5. "CIA's Secret Funding and the Constitution."

6. Rees, "Recent Developments regarding the Freedom of Information Act," 1185.

7. Milton Bearden quoted in Weiner, *Legacy of Ashes*, 431.

8. Raum, "CIA Recruiting Drive Paying Off."

9. Aftergood, "Intelligence Budget Data."

10. Harold Ford quoted in Weiner, *Legacy of Ashes*, 432.

11. Weiner, *Legacy of Ashes*, 432.

12. *Report of the Commission on Protecting and Reducing Government Secrecy.*

13. Ibid.

14. Gates, "Internal Memorandum on the Task Force for Greater Openness."

15. Ibid.

16. Ibid.

17. Ibid.

18. Ibid.

19. Kent Harrington, phone interview with the author, December 15, 2009.

20. Quoted in Carr, "Aldrich Ames and the Conduct of American Intelligence," 20.

21. Ibid.

22. Ibid., 19.

23. Harrington, phone interview with the author.

24. Ibid.

25. Ibid.

26. Powers, "One G-Man's Family," 485.

27. Robb, "Special Report: J. Edgar Hoover's Hollywood Obsessions Revealed."

28. Powers, "One G-Man's Family," 485–486.

29. Jeff Cohen, "*The Agency* on CBS."

30. Powers, "One G-Man's," 486.

31. Jack Myers, phone interview with the author, December 1, 2009.

32. Ibid.

33. Ibid.

34. Ibid.

35. David Houle, phone interview with the author, November 23, 2009.

36. Ibid.

37. Ibid.

38. Boxx, "CIA Television Series."

39. Ibid.

40. Myers, phone interview with the author.

41. Boxx, "CIA Television Series."

42. Ibid.

43. Myers, phone interview with the author.

44. Ibid.

45. Boxx, "CIA Television Series."

46. Spelling is listed in one of the CIA memos as working on the project for Fox, but neither Myers nor Houle remembered him being involved.

47. "CIA Television Series Project."

48. Ibid.

49. Houle, phone interview with the author.

50. Ibid.

51. "CIA Television Series Project."

52. Myers, phone interview with the author.

53. Ibid.

54. Houle, phone interview with the author.

55. Harrington, phone interview with the author.

56. Ibid.

57. Cohen, "*The Agency* on CBS."

58. As a further example, consider that Hoover used the popularity of his series to exert control over ABC's news division in November 1970. According to David Robb's "Media Jobs, Rights Under FBI Thumb," the news anchor Frank Reynolds mocked the Bureau's director on the air for his inability to handle criticism, causing Hoover to threaten to pull *The F.B.I.* unless Reynolds was fired. Given that the series regularly ranked in the top five of the Nielsen ratings, ABC relented and replaced Reynolds with Harry Reasoner.

59. Myers and Houle, phone interviews with the author.

60. Harlow, personal interview with the author, January 22, 2010.

61. Ibid.

62. Jenkins, "How the Central Intelligence Agency Works with Hollywood," 491.

63. Ibid.

64. Chase Brandon quoted in Robb, *Operation Hollywood*, 150.

65. Ibid.

66. Paul Barry quoted in Jenkins, "How the Central Intelligence Agency Works with Hollywood," 492.

67. Ibid.

68. Ibid.

69. Paul Barry, personal interview with the author, March 3, 2008.

70. "Now Playing Archive," *CIA.gov*, https://www.cia.gov/offices-of-cia/public-affairs/entertainment-industry-liaison/now-playing-archive.html.

71. Harlow, personal interview with the author.

72. Ibid.

73. Michael Sands, phone interview with the author, January 6, 2010.

74. Cruise/Wagner Productions did not end up producing the film, which was released in 2010. Instead, the role of Edwin A. Salt was changed to Evelyn A. Salt and played by Angelina Jolie. Columbia Pictures in association with Relativity Media produced the picture.

75. Michael Sands, e-mail to the author, May 17, 2010.

76. Van der Reijden, "Summer Camp Like the Bohemian Grove."

77. Alford and Graham, "Lights, Camera."

78. Sutel, "It's Not All Play at Media Conference"; Kirkpatrick, "Moguls Bicker and Brainstorm at Summer Camp"; Estulin, *True Story of the Bilderberg Group*.

79. Matt Corman and Chris Ord, phone interview with the author, July 27, 2010.

80. Ibid.

81. Andreeva, "USA Picks Up 'Covert Affairs' for Season 2." These statistics were calculated in August 2010.

82. Corman and Ord, phone interview with the author.

83. Ibid.

84. *Covert Affairs* is an upbeat representation of the CIA, which is depicted as full of competent, caring, and efficient officers engaged in dangerous, morally complicated, but ultimately rewarding work.

85. For instance, as David Robb noted in an e-mail to the author on February 24, 2010, he was able to acquire more than a thousand pages of notes, including details of script changes from the "very transparent and cooperative" marine corps film office in Los Angeles that detailed how the Pentagon shaped and censored Hollywood scripts. Additionally Phil Strub has donated hundreds of thousands of pages of the Pentagon's notes and correspondence with producers—going back fifty years—to Georgetown University's Special Collections archive. Strub also gave Lawrence Suid, a researcher sympathetic to the DOD, access to the Pentagon's more recent (post-1985) files. The CIA, however, very rarely leaves a paper trail, and Freedom of Information Act requests have yet to reveal anything of substance.

86. Bernstein, "The CIA and the Media."

Chapter 3

1. McCaslin, "Inside the Beltway."

2. Central Intelligence Agency, "DCI Meets Director of *The Agency*."

3. Bill Harlow, personal interview with the author, January 22, 2010.

4. Ibid.

5. Central Intelligence Agency, "*The Agency*'s Lead Characters Visit Headquarters."

6. Central Intelligence Agency, "Actress Alice Krige Visits Headquarters."

7. Ibid.

8. Brandon, "Lights . . . Camera."

9. Ibid.

10. Central Intelligence Agency, "Agency Hosts Movie Premier and Sneak Preview."

11. Central Intelligence Agency, "*The Agency* Gets the Green Light."

12. Michael Frost Beckner, phone interview with the author, December 2, 2009.

13. Ibid.

14. Tenet, *At the Center of the Storm*, 107.

15. Ibid.

16. Raum, "CIA Recruiting Drive Paying Off."

17. Harlow, personal interview with the author.

18. Central Intelligence Agency, "Agency Hosts Movie Premier and Sneak Preview."

19. Brandon, "Lights . . . Camera."

20. Harlow, personal interview with the author.

21. This line was likely influenced by Chase Brandon. As chapter 4 reveals, one of Brandon's major talking points was that while the CIA's failures are known, its successes are not—a convenient argument to deflect criticism since the CIA can suggest that its successes far outnumber its failures without ever having to provide evidence to support the claim.

22. Landers, "CIA Sees Dramatic Rise in Number of Applications."

23. "9/11 by the Numbers."

24. Lumpkin, "CIA Gets Big Boost in Bush Budget."

25. Knightley, "Miserable Failure Leaves Spies out in the Cold."

26. Goodman, "Revamping the CIA."

27. Goldstein, "CIA Spins Itself."

28. Cockburn, "Wide World of Torture."

29. Alan Dershowitz quoted in Farmer, "Debate Arises over Torture."

30. Bazzel Baz, phone interview with the author, November 9, 2009.

31. Beckner, phone interview with the author.

32. The original pilot episode for *The Agency* mentioned both Bin Laden and al-Qaeda by name. In the episode that actually aired, the reference to Bin Laden was removed due to the sensitivity surrounding the 9/11 attacks.

33. Harlow, personal interview with the author.

34. Beckner, phone interview with the author.

35. Ibid.

36. Breznican, "Mission Impossible?"
37. Ibid.
38. Richard Lindhelm quoted in Edwards, "Interview: Richard Lindhelm of the Institute for Creative Technologies."
39. Ibid.
40. Slagle, "Military Recruits Video Game Makers."
41. Beckner, phone interview with the author, March 3, 2010.
42. Tracey Rabb quoted in Silverman, "Fictional Anthrax Hits *The Agency.*"
43. "Two *Agency* Episodes May Not Air Due to Terrorism References."
44. Strum, "Spotlight; The C.I.A. as (Surprise!) the Good Guys."
45. Daniel Fierman quoted in Flaherty, "What to Watch."
46. Campbell, "*Company of Spies*; Inside Washington."
47. Grove, "Everything Old Is New Again."
48. Lapham, "The Boys Next Door."
49. Hall, "Encoding, Decoding."

Chapter 4

1. Chase Brandon quoted in Young, "Spook Shows."
2. John Rizzo quoted in *A Strange Bond: CIA and the Cinema.*
3. I transcribed this video, which Paul Barry showed to me when I visited the CIA on March 4, 2008.
4. Central Intelligence Agency, "New Recruitment Video on the CIA Careers Site."
5. Chase Brandon quoted in Grossberg, "Garner on Assignment for CIA."
6. Bill Harlow, personal interview with the author, January 22, 2010.
7. "Primetime Series."
8. Random House, "Bantam Books to Publish Official Companion and Fiction Series."
9. In the fight against terrorism, the show's CIA continually bordered on carrying out terrorist activity itself. During the series run, the Agency helps the U.S. government imprison and torture Sydney when it needs information stored in her brain, and employs techniques like the Inferno Protocol, which is an interrogation procedure that causes cardiac arrest in 50 percent of its subjects.
10. Sutherland and Swan, "The Good, the Bad, and the Justified," 131.
11. Cofer Black quoted in Schell, "When the Gloves Come Off."
12. Ibid.
13. Kean and Hamilton, *9/11 Report*, 590.
14. Ibid., 583.
15. Burke's character may have been partly based on Brandon himself, as he spent over two decades working in covert operations and then went on to serve as trainer at The Farm. Likewise, both Brandon and Burke were nearing the end of their careers at the CIA, trying to figure out how to secure their financial futures.
16. Butler, "Nearly All-Access Granted."
17. Harlow, personal interview with the author.
18. Ibid.

19. The source for this is Yasmin Naficy, who met with Chase Brandon to secure his assistance for her film *The Rogue* (preproduction); she spoke with me over the phone on April 28, 2010.

20. Kaur, "Recruits Get Glimpse of Secret CIA World."

21. "Premiere of Touchstone Pictures/Spyglass Entertainment's The Recruit."

22. Chase Brandon quoted in Paramount Pictures, "*The Sum of All Fears*."

23. Tom Berenger quoted in Burns, "CIA Given 'Human Face' by Hollywood."

24. Roger Birnbaum quoted in ibid.

25. Sailer, "*The Recruit*."

26. For instance, in *Clear and Present Danger*, an ailing Greer stresses that the deputy director of intelligence does not answer to the president of the United States; rather, he answers to the president's boss—the American citizens. This reminder encourages Ryan to testify before a congressional oversight committee about the unethical and secret operations in Colombia carried out by the CIA, the president, and the national security adviser, despite the fact that such testimony may endanger Ryan's career. Ryan and Greer, in other words, are constructed as the only non-corrupt government officials in the film, holding themselves accountable to Americans and refusing to be motivated by political self-interest.

27. The producers of *Patriot Games* were allowed to film a scene on the Langley campus, but the CIA refused to offer advice or guidance to the film's screenwriter, Peter Iliff, even though he, Tom Clancy, and the producer Mace Neufeld all petitioned the Agency for help.

28. Harlow, personal interview with the author.

29. Seelye, "When Hollywood's Big Guns Come Right from the Source."

30. The most clear representation of the inner-agency nemesis occurs in *Clear and Present Danger*, which features Robert Ritter, the CIA's deputy director of operations, and James Cutter, the national security adviser, working against Ryan on a covert operation. Marty Cantor in *Patriot Games* also plays an inner-agency nemesis to Ryan, although his actions are not nearly as egregious as Ritter's.

31. Department of the Navy, "Public Affairs Guidance."

32. Joint Staff, "Public Affairs."

33. Rainer, "Sister Act."

34. LaSalle, "No Escape."

35. Taylor, "Tom Clancy's Bogus Big-Bang Theory."

36. Paramount Pictures, "*The Sum of All Fears*."

37. Ibid.

38. Paramount Pictures, "*The Sum of All Fears*."

39. Taylor, "Tom Clancy's Bogus Big-Bang Theory."

40. Ebert, "*The Sum of All Fears*."

41. Paramount Pictures, "*The Sum of All Fears*."

42. John Strauchs, phone interview with the author, April 28, 2010.

43. Biersdorfer, "Hollywood's Gadget Factories."

44. Kaur, "Recruits Get Glimpse of Secret CIA World."

45. Strauchs, phone interview with the author.

46. Koltnow, "CIA Tries to Get It Right on Screen."

47. Michael Beckner, personal interview with the author, December 2, 2009.

48. Nicholas Dujmovic, e-mail to the author, March 10, 2010.

49. *"Enemy of the State."*

50. Ibid.

51. Peter Earnest, phone interview with the author, April 23, 2010.

52. Dujmovic, e-mail to the author.

53. Bowden and Daugherty in *A Strange Bond*. The idea of the CIA as an omnipresent power persists even today, as evidenced by several conspiracy theorists' blogs, which speculate that the CIA caused the 2010 Haitian and Chilean earthquakes, and by reports of Hugo Chavez likewise blaming the U.S. government for causing the Haitian earthquake by testing a "tectonic weapon" in an attempt to occupy the Caribbean.

54. Rizzo quoted in *A Strange Bond*.

55. Bart and Fleming, "Strangest PR Call of the Year."

56. Bierly, "Mike Myers Visits the CIA."

57. Paula Weiss, phone interview with the author, April 9, 2010.

58. Harlow, personal interview with the author.

59. Porter, *"Covert Affairs."*

60. Wiebe, *"Covert Affairs."*

61. As with everything of this nature, strong corroborating evidence from multiple sources is difficult to come by; but Sands did fax me evidence of his claims, including a legal document Abbas had signed indicating his consent to the interview.

Chapter 5

1. Abrams has argued many First Amendment cases before the Supreme Court, is the author of *Speaking Freely: Trials of the First Amendment*, and worked on the Pentagon Papers case.

2. Floyd Abrams quoted in Robb, *Operation Hollywood*, 47.

3. Ibid.

4. Erwin Chemerinsky quoted in ibid.

5. Anthony Kennedy quoted in ibid., 48.

6. Jenkins, "How the Central Intelligence Agency Works with Hollywood," 491.

7. Chase Brandon quoted in Farhi, "Speaking of Spooky."

8. Chase Brandon quoted in Young, "Spook Shows."

9. Michael Frost Beckner, phone interview with the author, December 2, 2009.

10. Chase Brandon quoted in Black, "Showbiz Gossip."

11. Chase Brandon quoted in Farhi, "Speaking of Spooky."

12. Paul Barry quoted in Jenkins, "How the Central Intelligence Agency Works with Hollywood," 494.

13. Ibid.

14. Paul Kelbaugh in *A Strange Bond*.

15. Ibid.

16. Ibid.

17. This point was, unsurprisingly, never addressed during the panel discussion hosted by the National Security Forum at William Mitchell College in 2007. When I asked Kelbaugh in a personal e-mail on March 4, 2010, about how the CIA reconciled its decisions with free speech issues, he failed to respond, even though he claimed in another e-mail, on February 23, 2010, to be "privy to a conversation with CIA Director George Tenet when THE decision [to work with Hollywood] was actually made."

18. John Rizzo and Paul Kelbaugh in *A Strange Bond*.

19. Robb, *Operation Hollywood*, 47–48.

20. This prohibition appears in numerous public laws, but the earliest is the Labor-Federal Security Appropriation Act of 1952. In 2003, an amended version of this law was passed, which prohibited agencies from using appropriated funds for publicity or propaganda purposes *within the United States* only.

21. The laws also prohibit the use of purely partisan communication, which the Justice Department defines as those publications that are "completely devoid of any connection with official functions" or "completely political in nature." The GAO has also characterized information as purely partisan when materials are found to have been designed to aid a political party or candidate, or are so political in nature that they do not further any of the purposes for which their government funds were appropriated. See, for instance, Bradbury, "Expenditure of Appropriated Funds for Informational Video and News Releases."

22. Gordon, "Department of Defense."

23. Koffsky, "General Services Administration Use of Government Funds for Advertising."

24. Ibid.

25. Tom Armstrong, phone interview with the author, March 22, 2010.

26. Senator Harry Byrd quoted in Bradbury, "Expenditure of Appropriated Funds for Informational Video News Releases."

27. Joel Timmer, personal interview with the author, April 29, 2010.

28. See "Comments on Lobbying and Propaganda Activities of the Office for Public Diplomacy for Latin America and the Caribbean"; and Pless, "B-211373.2, Jun 30, 1988."

29. Timmer, personal interview with the author.

30. Emphasis mine. Kent Harrington, phone interview with the author, December 15, 2009.

31. "CIA Names New Entertainment Liaison."

32. Paul Barry quoted in Jenkins, "How the Central Intelligence Agency Works with Hollywood," 494.

33. George Tenet quoted in Sciolino, "Cameras Are Being Turned on a Once-Shy Spy Agency."

34. Chase Brandon quoted in Bernstein, "Hardest-Working Actor of the Season."

35. Ibid.

36. Williams, "Chase Brandon."

37. Paul Barry, personal interview with the author, March 4, 2008.

38. See, for instance, Ryan, "License to Kill?"

39. Beckner, phone interview with the author.

40. Paul Kelbaugh in *A Strange Bond*. Please note that Kelbaugh does not refer to Huffstutler by name in his talk, but according to CIA historians, Huffstutler was executive director at the time.

41. Ibid.

42. Ibid.

43. Peter Iliff, e-mail to the author, March 28, 2010.

44. It should be noted that ultimately the CIA did not offer significant assistance to *Clear and Present Danger*, since CIA leadership is presented in an even uglier light than it was in *Patriot Games* (see chapter 1). But the CIA did agree to consider giving its cooperation and to review the script for the film, something Huffstutler refused to do for *Patriot Games*.

45. Chase Brandon quoted in Williams, "Chase Brandon."

46. Chase Brandon quoted in "Cloak and Dagger."

47. Regarding the CIA's destruction of interrogation tapes, see Mazzetti, "C.I.A. Destroyed 2 Tapes Showing Interrogations." Regarding the CIA's outsourcing of its intelligence gathering, see Ignatius, "When the CIA's Intelligence-Gathering Isn't Enough."

48. Robert Baer, phone interview with the author, December 31, 2009.

49. Chase Brandon quoted in Robb, *Operation Hollywood*, 152.

50. Welch, "Introduction: Propaganda in Historical Perspective," xix.

51. David Culbert quoted in Giglio, *Here's Looking at You*, 59.

52. John Rizzo in *A Strange Bond*.

53. Strub, letter to Centropolis Entertainment.

54. Devlin, letter to Phil Strub.

55. Baer, phone interview with the author.

56. Noam Chomsky in "On Propaganda."

57. Ibid.

58. Noam Chomsky in *Manufacturing Consent* (DVD).

59. Diamond, *The CIA and the Culture of Failure*, 21.

60. Ibid., 404.

61. Ibid., 405.

62. Marlin, *Propaganda and the Ethics of Persuasion*, 95.

63. Ibid.

64. "Tom Boosts CIA Image," 4.

65. Michael Sands, personal interview with the author, January 6, 2010.

66. See, for instance, "The CIA's Man in Hollywood"; and Newman, "Every Second Counts."

67. "Payola and Sponsorship Identification."

68. Koltnow, "CIA Tries to Get It Right on Screen."

69. Doyle, "End of Secrecy," 45–46.

70. Aftergood, "Intelligence Budget Data."

71. Ivan Eland quoted in Katharine Seelye, "When Hollywood's Big Guns Come Right from the Source."

Chapter 6

1. Bazzel Baz, phone interview with the author, November 9, 2009.
2. Robert Baer, phone interview with the author, December 31, 2009.
3. Ibid.
4. See, for instance, Willing, "Spy Books Strain CIA Review Board." In it, Willing highlights the dramatic increase in the number of current or former spies submitting material for approval by the CIA's Publications Review Board (a requirement for all Agency employees turned writers). In 1980, the board received fewer than one hundred manuscripts, totaling about ten thousand pages. In 2000, they received three hundred manuscripts, totaling about fifteen thousand pages. By 2004, they reviewed more than four hundred and fifty manuscripts, totaling about thirty thousand pages. In 2007, the board received an average of one hundred manuscripts *per month*, totaling thousands of pages each month. According to Kent Harrington, "It's a safe bet that [these numbers] are also a good measure of the large number, some subset of this group, who have either taken or are seeking to take their tales to Hollywood." Kent Harrington, phone interview with the author, December 15, 2009.
5. Ibid.
6. Ibid.
7. Paul Barry, personal interview with the author, March 3, 2008.
8. Harrington, phone interview with the author.
9. Although AMC invited Mendez to its studios to comment on the topic, Mendez's commentary was not used in the final version of the program. He claims this was because he told the program that there was no conspiracy to control Middle Eastern oil — an argument AMC did not want to hear. His nonappearance on the program does not seem to have been affected by his fields of expertise.
10. Hersh is quoted as saying this in promotional material for Baer's book *See No Evil: The True History of a Ground Soldier in the CIA's War on Terrorism*.
11. Ketcham, "Unlearning the CIA."
12. Baer, *See No Evil*, 6–7.
13. Ketcham, "Unlearning the CIA."
14. Siegel, "Ex-CIA Agent Robert Baer, Inspiration for 'Syriana.'"
15. Rocchi, "Interview: Stephen Gaghan, Director and Writer of *Syriana*."
16. Lawrence, "I Want My Movie to Offend Absolutely Everyone."
17. Ibid.
18. Baer, phone interview with the author.
19. *The Wire* was cowritten by a former homicide investigator and police journalist and has often been hailed as one of the most authentic police programs of all time.
20. Rozen, "Hollywood and the CIA."
21. Ibid.
22. Additionally, Bearden has served as a media contributor, appearing in several documentaries, writing op-ed pieces in the *New York Times* and the *Wall Street Journal*, and working as a consultant for CBS News.
23. Luce, "Retired CIA Agent/Author Milton Bearden Talks *The Good Shepherd*."

24. Ibid.

25. Ibid.

26. "*The Good Shepherd*: Eric Roth (Screenwriter)."

27. Ibid.

28. Milt Bearden quoted in Luce, "Retired CIA Agent/Author Milton Bearden Talks *The Good Shepherd*."

29. Ibid.

30. Paul Barry quoted in Argetsinger and Roberts, "CIA Has a New Man on a Special Mission."

31. Dujmovic, "Hollywood, Don't You Go Disrespectin' My Culture," 26.

32. Paul Barry criticized *The Good Shepherd* in Argetsinger and Roberts's article in the *Washington Post*. Nicholas Dujmovic lambasted the same film in an article for *Intelligence and National Security*, which he also presented in a lecture series at the David M. Kennedy Center for International Studies at Brigham Young University. Likewise, the CIA general counsel John Rizzo, in a panel discussion held at William Mitchell College of Law in 2007, derided *Syriana* for failing to base its events on actual history. Rizzo's talk is available on the *Strange Bond* DVD.

33. Herman and Chomsky, *Manufacturing Consent*, 27.

34. Jenkins, "How the Central Intelligence Agency Works with Hollywood," 492.

35. Hoffer and Nelson, "Docudrama on American Television," 65.

36. Leslie Woodhead quoted in Rosenthal, "Introduction," xv.

37. Rozen, "Hollywood and the CIA."

38. Frazer, "A Little More Than Luck on *Syriana* and *Good Night, and Good Luck*."

39. Faraci, "Interview: Robert Baer."

40. Ibid.

41. Siegel, "Ex-CIA Agent Robert Baer, Inspiration for 'Syriana.'"

42. John Rizzo in *A Strange Bond*.

43. Tony Mendez, personal interview with the author, March 4, 2008.

44. Rosenstone, "*JFK*: Historical Fact/Historical Film," 338.

45. Crowdus, "Living in a Wilderness of Mirrors," 14.

46. See http://www.thegoodshepherdmovie.com/.

47. Dujmovic, "Hollywood, Don't You Go Disrespectin' My Culture."

48. Robarge et al., "Intelligence in Public Media."

49. Rosenstone, "*JFK*: Historical Fact/Historical Film," 333.

50. Ibid., 334.

51. Ibid., 336.

52. Ibid., 337.

53. Ibid., 339.

54. Woodhead, "Guardian Lecture," 109.

55. Rosenthal, "Introduction," 8.

56. Ibid.

57. Rosenstone, "The Historical Film," 56.

58. Dujmovic, "Hollywood, Don't You Go Disrespectin' My Culture," 26.

59. Baer, phone interview with the author; and Paul Barry quoted in Jenkins, "How the Central Intelligence Agency Works with Hollywood," 492.

Conclusion

1. Suid, *"Operation Hollywood."*

2. Ibid.

3. Barry quoted in Jenkins, "How the Central Intelligence Agency Works with Hollywood," 494.

4. Paula Weiss, phone interview with the author, April 9, 2010.

5. Paul Barry, personal interview with the author, March 4, 2008.

6. Weiss, phone interview with the author, April 9, 2010.

Bibliography

Abrams, Floyd. *Speaking Freely: Trials of the First Amendment*. New York: Viking, 2005.

Aftergood, Steve. "Intelligence Budget Data." FAS.org, n.d. http://www.fas.org/irp/budget/index.html.

Aldrich, Richard. "Regulation by Revelation? Intelligence, the Media, and Transparency." In *Spinning Intelligence*, edited by Robert Dover and Michael Goodman, 13–36. New York: Columbia University Press, 2009.

Alford, Matthew, and Robbie Graham. "Lights, Camera . . . Covert Action." *Global Research: Center for Research on Globalization*, January 21, 2009. http://www.globalresearch.ca/index.php?context=va&aid=11921.

American Civil Liberties Union. "Celebrities Speak Out for Civil Liberties in New ACLU Advertising Campaign." ACLU.org, September 15, 2003. http://www.aclu.org/national-security/celebrities-speak-out-civil-liberties-new-aclu-advertising-campaign.

Andreeva, Nellie. "USA Picks Up 'Covert Affairs' for Season 2." Deadline.com, August 18, 2010. http://www.deadline.com/2010/08/usa-network-picks-up-covert-affairs-for-a-second-season/.

Argetsinger, Amy, and Roxanne Roberts. "The CIA Has a New Man on a Special Mission—to Hollywood." *Washington Post*, June 5, 2007. http://www.washingtonpost.com/wp-dyn/content/article/2007/06/04/AR2007060402111.html.

Baer, Robert. *See No Evil: The True Story of a Ground Soldier in the CIA's War on Terrorism*. New York: Three Rivers Press, 2002.

———. *Sleeping with the Devil: How Washington Sold Our Soul for Saudi Crude*. New York: Three Rivers Press, 2003.

Barrett, David. *The CIA and Congress: The Untold Story from Truman to Kennedy*. Lawrence: University Press of Kansas, 2005.

Bart, Peter, and Michael Fleming. "Strangest PR Call of the Year: The CIA." *Variety*, December 19, 2009. http://weblogs.variety.com/hal/2008/12/strangest-pr-ca.html.

Bearden, Milt. *Black Tulip: A Novel of War in Afghanistan*. New York: Random House, 1998.

Bearden, Milt, and James Risen. *The Main Enemy: The Inside Story of the CIA's Final Showdown with the KGB*. New York: Random House, 2003.

Bernstein, Carl. "The CIA and the Media." *Rolling Stone*, October 20, 1977. http://www.carlbernstein.com/magazine_cia_and_media.php.

Bernstein, Paula. "Hardest-Working Actor of the Season: The C.I.A." *New York Times*, September 2, 2001. http://www.nytimes.com/2001/09/02/arts/television-radio-hardest-working-actor-of-the-season-the-cia.html.

Bierly, Mandi. "Mike Myers Visits the CIA. Naturally." EW.com, May 12, 2009. http://popwatch.ew.com/2009/05/12/mike-myers-cia/.

Biersdorfer, J. D. "Hollywood's Gadget Factories." *New York Times*, September 26, 2002. http://www.nytimes.com/2002/09/26/technology/hollywood-s-gadget-factories.html.

Black, Zoe. "Showbiz Gossip: Features." *Wales on Sunday*, October 14, 2001. http://www.highbeam.com/doc/1G1-84891752.html.

Bolten, Joshua. "Enforcing the CIA's Secrecy Agreement through Postpublication Civil Action: *United States v. Snepp*." *Stanford Law Review* 32, no. 2 (January 1980): 409–531.

Boxx, Dennis. "CIA Television Series." CIA.gov, April 16, 1996. http://www.foia.cia.gov/docs/DOC_0001272789/DOC_0001272789.pdf.

Bradbury, Steven. "Expenditure of Appropriated Funds for Informational Video News Releases." U.S. Office of Legal Counsel, July 30, 2004. http://www.justice.gov/olc/opfinal.htm.

Brandon, Chase. "Lights . . . Camera . . . Action!" *What's News at CIA* 538 (September 2005). http://www.foia.cia.gov/docs/DOC_0001243289/DOC_0001243289.pdf.

Breznican, Anthony. "Mission Impossible? Not for Hollywood, CIA." *Chicago Sun-Times*, December 3, 2001. http://www.highbeam.com/doc/1P2-4619587.html.

Burns, Robert. "CIA Given 'Human Face' by Hollywood." Associated Press, October 14, 1999. http://www.mail-archive.com/ctrl@listserv.aol.com/msg26191.html.

Bushnell, William. "Paying for the Damage: *The Quiet American* Revisited." *Film & History* 36, no. 2 (Spring 2006): 38–44.

Butler, Tim. "Nearly All-Access Granted: The CIA Relaxes Its Closed-Door Policy for New Spy Thriller, *The Recruit*, Starring Al Pacino and Colin Farrell." *Tri-State Defender*, January 22, 2003. http://www.highbeam.com/doc/1P1-79656662.html.

Campbell, Matthew. "*Company of Spies*; Inside Washington." *Sunday Times*, October 10, 1999.

Carr, Caleb. "Aldrich Ames and the Conduct of American Intelligence." *World Policy Journal* 11, no. 3 (Fall 1994): 19–28.

Central Intelligence Agency. "About CIA." CIA.gov, April 19, 2007. https://www.cia.gov/about-cia/.

———. "Actress Alice Krige Visits Headquarters." *What's News at CIA* 532 (September 2005). http://www.foia.cia.gov/docs/DOC_0001243425/DOC_0001243425.pdf.

———. "*The Agency* Gets the Green Light." *What's News at CIA* 822 (May 17, 2001). http://www.foia.cia.gov/docs/DOC_0001243419/DOC_0001243419.pdf.

————. "Agency Hosts Movie Premier and Sneak Preview." *What's News at CIA* 683 (September 2005). http://www.foia.cia.gov/docs/DOC_0001243292/DOC_0001243292.pdf.

————. "*The Agency*'s Lead Characters Visit Headquarters." *What's News at CIA* 528 (September 2005). http://www.foia.cia.gov/docs/DOC_0001243415/DOC_0001243415.pdf.

————. "DCI Meets Director of *The Agency*." *What's News at CIA* 519 (September 2005). http://www.foia.cia.gov/docs/DOC_0001243293/DOC_0001243293.pdf.

————. "New Recruitment Video on the CIA Careers Site." CIA.gov, March 8, 2004. https://www.cia.gov/news-information/press-releases-statements/press-release-archive-2004/pr03082004.html.

————. "Support to Mission." CIA.gov, May 24, 2007. https://www.cia.gov/offices-of-cia/mission-support/organization.html.

"The CIA's Man in Hollywood." ABCNews.com, November 29, 2005. http://abcnews.go.com/GMA/story?id=1355027.

"CIA Names New Entertainment Liaison." CIA.gov, June 5, 2007. https://www.cia.gov/news-information/press-releases-statements/cia-names-new-entertainment-liaison.html.

"The CIA's Secret Funding and the Constitution." *Yale Law Journal* 84, no. 3 (1975): 608–636.

"CIA Television Series Project." CIA.gov, October 3, 2005. http://www.foia.cia.gov/docs/DOC_0001243414/DOC_0001243414.pdf.

"Cloak and Dagger." *The Bourne Identity (Widescreen Extended Edition)*, DVD. Directed by Doug Liman. Universal City, CA: Universal Studios, 2004.

Cockburn, Alexander. "The Wide World of Torture." *The Nation*, November 26, 2001. http://www.thenation.com/article/wide-world-torture.

Cohen, Jeff. "*The Agency* on CBS: Right Time but Wrong Show." FAIR.org, October 8, 2001. http://www.fair.org/index.php?page=2464.

"Comments on Lobbying and Propaganda Activities of the Office for Public Diplomacy for Latin America and the Caribbean." U.S. Government Accountability Office, September 30, 1987. http://www.gao.gov/products/134174.

"Could the Gov/CIA Have Caused This Earthquake/Tsunami?" *Able2Know*, January 1, 2005. http://able2know.org/topic/42148-1.

Crowdus, Gary. "Living in a Wilderness of Mirrors: An Interview with Eric Roth." *Cineaste* 32, no. 3 (Summer 2007): 14–19.

De Cristofaro, Maria, and Sebastian Rotella. "Italy Judge Convicts 23 Americans in 2003 CIA Kidnapping of Egyptian Cleric." *Los Angeles Times*, November 4, 2009. http://articles.latimes.com/2009/nov/05/world/fg-italy-verdict5.

Department of the Navy. "Public Affairs Guidance: Navy Production Assistance to *The Hunt for Red October*." February 1990. Available through the Gwendolyn P. Tandy Memorial Film Library's Government in Hollywood Special Collection at Texas Christian University, Fort Worth, TX.

Devlin, Dean. Letter to Phil Strub. May 8, 1995. Available through the Gwendolyn P. Tandy Memorial Film Library's Government in Hollywood Special Collection at Texas Christian University, Fort Worth, TX.

Diamond, John. *The CIA and the Culture of Failure: U.S. Intelligence from the End of the Cold War to the Invasion of Iraq*. Stanford, CA: Stanford University Press, 2008.

Douglas, Edward. "*Rendition* Writer Kelley Sane." ComingSoon.net, October 18, 2007. http://www.comingsoon.net/news/movienews.php?id=38328.

Doyle, Kate. "The End of Secrecy: U.S. National Security and the Imperative for Openness." *World Policy Journal* 16, no. 1 (1999): 34–51.

Doyle, Kate, and Peter Kornbluh. "CIA and Assassinations: The Guatemala 1954 Documents." *National Security Archive Electronic Briefing Book No. 4*, *n.d.* http://www.gwu.edu/~nsarchiv/NSAEBB/NSAEBB4/.

Dujmovic, Nicholas. "'Hollywood, Don't You Go Disrespectin' My Culture': *The Good Shepherd* versus Real CIA History." *Intelligence and National Security* 23, no. 1 (2008): 25– 41.

———. "Two CIA Prisoners in China, 1952–73." *Studies in Intelligence* 50, no. 4 (2006). https://www.cia.gov/library/center-for-the-study-of-intelligence/csi-publications/csi-studies/studies/vol50no4/two-cia-prisoners-in-china-1952201373.html.

Earley, Pete. *Confessions of a Spy: The Real Story of Aldrich Ames*. New York: Berkley, 1998.

Ebert, Roger. "*The Sum of All Fears*." RogerEbert.com, May 31, 2002. http://rogerebert.suntimes.com/apps/pbcs.dll/article?AID=/20020531/REVIEWS/205310302/1023.

Edwards, Bob. "Interview: Richard Lindhelm of the Institute for Creative Technologies, Talks about Hollywood's Brainstorming with the Military." *Morning Edition: NPR*, October 15, 2001.

Eldridge, David. "'Dear Owen': The CIA, Luigi Luraschi, and Hollywood, 1953." *Historical Journal of Film, Radio, and Television* 20, no. 2 (June 2000): 149–196.

"*Enemy of the State*." *Columbus (GA) Times*, November 24, 1998. http://www.highbeam.com/doc/1P1-22128329.html.

Estulin, Daniel. *The True Story of the Bilderberg Group*. Walterville, OR: Trine Day, 2007.

"Executive Order 12333—United States Intelligence Activities." U.S. National Archives: Federal Register, December 4, 1981. http://www.archives.gov/federal-register/codification/executive-order/12333.html.

Faraci, Devin. "Interview: Robert Baer." *Free Republic*, November 20, 2005. http://www.freerepublic.com/focus/news/1590834/posts.

Farhi, Paul. "Speaking of Spooky: TV's New Spy Crop; Networks Uncover Huge Cache of Series with Help of Heroic Federal Agencies." *Washington Post*, August 4, 2001. http://www.highbeam.com/doc/1P2-456123.html.

Farmer, Tom. "Debate Arises over Torture." *Boston Herald*, January 22, 2002.

Flaherty, Mike. "What to Watch." *Entertainment Weekly*, October 22, 1999. http://www.ew.com/ew/article/0,,271275,00.html.

Flintoff, Corey. "How Far Did CIA Assassination Plans Go?" National Public Radio, June 14, 2009. http://www.npr.org/templates/story/story.php?storyId=106597830.

Frazer, Bryant. "A Little More Than Luck on *Syriana* and *Good Night, and Good Luck*." *Film & Video*, January 1, 2006. http://www.studiodaily.com/filmandvideo/projects/f/movies/5857.html.

Gates, Robert. "Internal Memorandum on the Task Force for Greater Openness." *CIA on Campus*, Winter 1991. http://www.cia-on-campus.org/foia/pao1.html.

Giglio, Ernest. *Here's Looking at You: Hollywood, Film, and Politics*. New York: Peter Lang, 2005.

Goldstein, Patrick. "The CIA Spins Itself." *Los Angeles Times*, September 29, 2001. http://articles.latimes.com/2001/sep/29/entertainment/ca-51174.

Goodman, Melvin. "Revamping the CIA: The Terrorist Attacks Have Once Again Exposed Wide-Ranging Flaws in the Agency's Operations." *Issues in Science and Technology* 18, no. 2 (December 22, 2001). http://www.issues.org/18.2/goodman.html.

"*The Good Shepherd*: Eric Roth (Screenwriter)." *Close-Up Film*, 2003. http://www.close-upfilm.com/features/Interviews/eric_roth.html.

Gordon, Daniel I. "Department of Defense-Retired Military Officers as Media Analysts." U.S. Government Accountability Office, July 21, 2009. http://www.gao.gov/decisions/appro/316443.pdf.

Green, Joey. *The "Get Smart" Handbook*. New York: Collier, 1993.

Gribble, Richard. "Anti-communism, Patrick Peyton, CSC, and the CIA." *Journal of Church and State* 45, no. 3 (June 2003): 535–58.

Grossberg, Josh. "Garner on Assignment for CIA." *E! Online*, August 28, 2003. http://www.eonline.com/uberblog/b45750_garner_on_assignment_cia.html.

Grove, David. "Everything Old Is New Again." PopMatters.com, n.d. http://www.popmatters.com/tv/reviews/a/agency.shtml.

"Haiti Earthquake Caused by Bush/Clinton Attack with Tesla." *Godlike Productions*, January 14, 2010. http://www.godlikeproductions.com/forum1/message964860/pg1.

Hall, Stuart. "Encoding, Decoding." In *The Cultural Studies Reader*, edited by Simon During, 507–18. London: Routledge, 1993.

Herman, Edward, and Noam Chomsky. *Manufacturing Consent: The Political Economy of the Mass Media*. New York: Pantheon Books, 2002.

Hersh, Seymour. "Huge CIA Operation Reported in U.S. against Anti-war Forces, Other Dissidents in Nixon Years." *New York Times*, December 22, 1974.

Hoffer, Tom, and Richard Nelson. "Docudrama on American Television." In *Why Docudrama? Fact-Fiction on Film and TV*, edited by Alan Rosenthal, 64–77. Carbondale: Southern Illinois University Press, 1999.

"Hugo Chavez Says U.S. Weapon Caused Haitian Earthquake." *News One*, January 21, 2010. http://newsone.com/world/news-one-staff/hugo-chavez-says-u-s-weapon-caused-haitian-earthquake/.

Ignatius, David. "When the CIA's Intelligence-Gathering Isn't Enough." *Washington Post*, March 18, 2010. http://www.washingtonpost.com/wp-dyn/content/article/2010/03/16/AR2010031602625.html.

Jenkins, Tricia. "Get Smart: A Look at the Current Relationship between Hollywood and the CIA." *Historical Journal of Film, Radio, and Television* 29, no. 2 (June 2009): 229–243.

———. "How the Central Intelligence Agency Works with Hollywood: An Interview with Paul Barry, the CIA's New Entertainment Industry Liaison." *Media, Culture, and Society* 31, no. 3 (May 2009): 489–495.

Joint Staff. "Public Affairs: Movie Premieres and Showings of *Hunt for Red Octo-*

ber." November 1989. Available through the Gwendolyn P. Tandy Memorial Film Library's Government in Hollywood Special Collection at Texas Christian University, Fort Worth, TX.

Kaur, Manveet. "Recruits Get Glimpse of Secret CIA World." *New Straits Times*, April 20, 2003. http://www.highbeam.com/doc/1P1-82788004.html.

Kean, Thomas, and Lee Hamilton. *The 9/11 Report: The National Commission on Terrorist Attacks upon the United States*. New York: St. Martin's Press, 2004.

Kessler, Ronald. *Inside the CIA: Revealing the Secrets of the World's Most Powerful Spy Agency*. New York: Pocket Books, 1994.

Ketcham, Christopher. "Unlearning the CIA: The Education of Bob Baer." *Pacific Free Press*, October 24, 2009. http://www.pacificfreepress.com/news/1/4936-the-education-of-bob-baer.html.

Kirkpatrick, David. "Moguls Bicker and Brainstorm at Summer Camp." *International Herald Tribune*, July 14, 2003. http://www.highbeam.com/doc/1P1-75219415.html.

Knightley, Phillip. "Miserable Failure Leaves Spies out in the Cold." *The Independent*, September 16, 2001. http://www.independent.co.uk/opinion/commentators/phillip-knightley-miserable-failure-leaves-spies-out-in-the-cold-669495.html.

Koffsky, Daniel. "General Services Administration Use of Government Funds for Advertising." U.S. Department of Justice, January 19, 2001. http://www.justice.gov/olc/gsafinal.htm.

Koltnow, Barry. "CIA Tries to Get It Right on Screen." *Orange County Register*, June 10, 2002. http://www.highbeam.com/doc/1G1-120284750.html.

Landers, Jim. "CIA Sees Dramatic Rise in Number of Applications for Employment." Knight Ridder/Tribune News Service, September 19, 2001. http://www.highbeam.com/doc/1G1-78416691.html.

Lapham, Lewis. "The Boys Next Door." *Harper's Magazine*, July 2001. http://www.harpers.org/archive/2001/07/0072377.

LaSalle, Mick. "No Escape: Clancy Thriller *Sum of All Fears* Hits a Little Too Close to Home." *San Francisco Chronicle*, May 31, 2002. http://www.sfgate.com/cgi-bin/article.cgi?f=/chronicle/reviews/movies/SUMOFALLFEARS.DTL.

Lawrence, Will. "I Want My Movie to Offend Absolutely Everyone." *Evening Standard*, December 22, 2005. http://www.highbeam.com/doc/1G1-140070411.html.

Leab, Daniel. *Orwell Subverted: The CIA and the Filming of "Animal Farm."* University Park: Pennsylvania State University Press, 2007.

Loeb, Vernon. "The CIA's Operation Hollywood: 'Company of Spies' Wins Raves from Image-Conscious Agency." *Washington Post*, October 14, 1999. http://www.fas.org/irp/news/1999/10/261l-101499-idx.htm.

Luce, Patrick. "Retired CIA Agent/Author Milton Bearden Talks *The Good Shepherd*." *Monsters and Critics*, March 30, 2007. http://www.monstersandcritics.com/dvd/features/article_1285004.php.

Lumpkin, John. "CIA Gets Big Boost in Bush Budget." Associated Press, February 5, 2002. http://www.highbeam.com/doc/1P1-49977236.html.

———. "U.S. Can Target American al-Qaida Agents." *Yahoo! News*, Decem-

ber 3, 2002. http://www.timeenoughforlove.org/saved/YahooNewsU_S_Can
TargetAmericanal-QaidaAgents.htm.

Lundegaard, Erik. "You're Not Reading This: CIA in Hollywood Movies." msnbc
.com, December 21, 2006. http://www.msnbc.msn.com/id/16270828/.

Manufacturing Consent: Noam Chomsky and the Media, DVD. Directed by Mark
Achbar and Peter Wintonick. New York: Zeitgeist Films, 2002.

Marlin, Randal. *Propaganda and the Ethics of Persuasion.* Peterborough, ON:
Broadview Press, 2002.

Mazzetti, Mark. "C.I.A. Destroyed 2 Tapes Showing Interrogations." *New York
Times,* December 7, 2007. http://www.nytimes.com/2007/12/07/washington/
07intel.html.

McCaslin, John. "Inside the Beltway." *Washington Times,* October 7, 1999. http://
www.highbeam.com/doc/1G1-58395825.html.

McGilligan, Patrick. "*Three Days of the Condor*: Sidney Pollack Interviewed."
Jump Cut 10/11 (1976). http://www.ejumpcut.org/archive/onlinessays/JC
10-11folder/PollackMcGilligan.html.

Mendez, Antonio. *Master of Disguise: My Secret Life inside the CIA.* New York:
William Morrow, 1999.

Miller, Greg. "CIA-Blackwater Assassination Contract Points to Larger Connections." *Los Angeles Times,* August 21, 2009. http://articles.latimes.com/2009/
aug/21/nation/na-cia-blackwater21.

Newman, Kathy. "Every Second Counts." *Pacific Northwest Inlander,* November 8,
2001. http://www.inlander.com/spokane/article-1120–every-second-counts
.html.

"9/11 by the Numbers." *New York Magazine,* April 4, 2007. http://nymag.com/
news/articles/wtc/1year/numbers.htm.

"Now Playing Archive." CIA.gov, October 2007–May 2008. https://www.cia
.gov/offices-of-cia/public-affairs/entertainment-industry-liaison/now-playing-
archive.html.

"On Propaganda: Noam Chomsky Interviewed by Unidentified Interviewer."
WBAI, January 1992. http://www.chomsky.info/interviews/199201—.htm.

Paramount Pictures. "*The Sum of All Fears*: Q&A with CIA Expert Chase
Brandon." *UGO.com,* n.d. http://www.ugo.com/channels/filmtv/features/
sumofallfears/chasebrandon.asp.

"Payola and Sponsorship Identification." U.S. Federal Communications Commission, September 30, 2010. http://www.fcc.gov/eb/broadcast/sponsid.html.

Pless, Don. "B-211373.2, Jun 30, 1988." U.S. Government Accountability Office,
n.d. http://redbook.gao.gov/13/fl0060110.php.

Porter, Rick. "*Covert Affairs*: How Valerie Plame Helped Doug Liman Make
the Show." Zap2It.com, July 10, 2010. http://blog.zap2it.com/frominsidethe-
box/2010/07/covert-affairs-how-valerie-plame-helped-doug-liman-make-the-
show.html.

Powers, Richard. "One G-Man's Family: Popular Entertainment Formulas
and J. Edgar Hoover's F.B.I." *American Quarterly* 30, no. 4 (Autumn 1978):
471–492.

"Premiere of Touchstone Pictures/Spyglass Entertainment's *The Recruit*." *PR*

Newswire, January 29, 2003. http://www.highbeam.com/doc/1G1-96987248
.html.

"Primetime Series." *Hollywood Reporter*, May 27, 2005. http://www.hollywood
reporter.com/hr/search/article_display.jsp?vnu_content_id=1000937471.

Rainer, Peter. "Sister Act." *New York Magazine*. June 10, 2001. http://nymag.com/
nymetro/movies/reviews/6082/.

Random House. "Bantam Books to Publish Official Companion and Fiction
Series Based on Hit ABC Television Show *Alias*." *PR Newswire*, June 10,
2002. http://www.thefreelibrary.com/ Bantam+Books+to+Publish+Official+
Companion+and+Fiction+Series+Based. . .-a087463841.

Raum, Tom. "CIA Recruiting Drive Paying Off." FAS.org, January 17, 2000.
http://www.fas.org/sgp/news/2000/01/ap011700.html.

Rees, Amy. "Recent Developments regarding the Freedom of Information Act:
A 'Prologue to a Farce or a Tragedy; Or, Perhaps Both.'" *Duke Law Journal* 44,
no. 6 (1995): 1183–1223.

Report of the Commission on Protecting and Reducing Government Secrecy, 1997. Washington, DC: U.S. Government Printing Office, 1997. http://www.gpo.gov/
congress/commissions/secrecy/index.html.

Robarge, David, Gary McCollim, Nicholas Dujmovic, and Thomas G. Coffey.
"Intelligence in Public Media: *The Good Shepherd*." *Studies in Intelligence* 50,
no. 1 (2007). https://www.cia.gov/library/center-for-the-study-of-intelligence/
csi-publications/csi-studies/studies/vol51no1/the-good-shepherd.html.

Robb, David. *Operation Hollywood: How the Pentagon Shapes and Censors the Movies*.
Amherst, NY: Prometheus Books, 2004.

———. "Media Jobs, Rights Under FBI Thumb in Secret History of TV Show."
Hollywood Today, February 28, 2008. http://www.hollywoodtoday.net/2008/02/
28/media-jobs-rights-under-fbi-thumb-in-secret-history-of-tv-show.

———. "Special Report: J. Edgar Hoover's Hollywood Obsessions Revealed." *Hollywood Today*, February 27, 2008. http://www.hollywoodtoday
.net/2008/02/27/special-report-j-edgar-hoover.

Rocchi, James. "Interview: Stephen Gaghan, Director and Writer of *Syriana*."
Cinematical, December 2, 2005. http://www.cinematical.com/2005/12/02/
interview-stephen-gaghan-director-and-writer-of-syriana/.

Rosenstone, Robert. "The Historical Film: Looking at the Past in a Postliterate
Age." In *The Historical Film: History and Memory in Media*, edited by Marcia
Landry, 50–66. New Brunswick, NJ: Rutgers University Press, 2001.

———. "*JFK*: Historical Fact/Historical Film." In *Why Docudrama? Fact-Fiction
on Film and TV*, edited by Alan Rosenthal, 333–39. Carbondale: Southern Illinois University Press, 1999.

Rosenthal, Alan. "Introduction." In *Why Docudrama? Fact-Fiction on Film and
TV*, edited by Alan Rosenthal, 1–11. Carbondale: Southern Illinois University Press, 1999.

Rositzke, Harry. *The CIA's Secret Operations: Espionage, Counterespionage, and
Covert Action*. Boulder, CO: Westview Press, 1988.

Rozen, Laura. "Hollywood and the CIA: The Spook Stays in the Picture."
Mother Jones, December 13, 2007. http://motherjones.com/politics/2007/12/
hollywood-and-cia-spook-stays-picture.

Ryan, Jason. "License to Kill? Intelligence Chief Says U.S. Can Take Out American Terrorists." ABCNews.com, February 3, 2010. http://abcnews.go.com/Politics/license-kill-intelligence-chief-us-american-terrorist/story?id=9740491.

Sailer, Steve. "*The Recruit.*" United Press International, January 30, 2003. http://www.isteve.com/Film_Recruit.htm.

Schell, Jonathan. "When the Gloves Come Off." *The Nation*, October 15, 2008. http://www.thenation.com/article/when-gloves-come.

Sciolino, Elaine. "Cameras Are Being Turned on a Once-Shy Spy Agency." *New York Times*, May 6, 2001. http://www.nytimes.com/2001/05/06/us/cameras-are-being-turned-on-a-once-shy-spy-agency.html.

Seelye, Katharine Q. "When Hollywood's Big Guns Come Right from the Source." *New York Times*, June 10, 2002. http://www.nytimes.com/2002/06/10/us/when-hollywood-s-big-guns-come-right-from-the-source.html?pagewanted=1.

Shaw, Tony. *Hollywood's Cold War*. Edinburgh: Edinburgh University Press, 2007.

Siegel, Robert. "Ex-CIA Agent Robert Baer, Inspiration for 'Syriana.'" *All Things Considered: NPR*, December 6, 2005. http://www.npr.org/templates/story/story.php?storyId=5041385.

Silverman, Stephen. "Fictional Anthrax Hits *The Agency*." *People*, November 6, 2001. http://www.people.com/people/article/0,,622900,00.html.

Slagle, Matt. "Military Recruits Video Game Makers." Associated Press, October 3, 2003. http://www.highbeam.com/doc/1P1-85377847.html.

"Spy School: Inside the CIA Training Program." *The Recruit*, DVD. Directed by Roger Donaldson. Written by Serena Yang. Burbank, CA: Touchstone Pictures, 2003.

A Strange Bond: CIA and the Cinema, DVD. St. Paul: William Mitchell College of Law, 2007.

Strub, Phil. Letter to Centropolis Entertainment. April 1995. Available through the Gwendolyn P. Tandy Memorial Film Library's Government in Hollywood Special Collection at Texas Christian University, Fort Worth, TX.

Strum, Charles. "Spotlight; The C.I.A. as (Surprise!) the Good Guys." *New York Times*, October 24, 1999. http://www.nytimes.com/1999/10/24/tv/spotlight-the-cia-as-surprise-the-good-guys.html.

Suid, Lawrence. "*Operation Hollywood*: An Exercise in Futility." *Film & History* 35, no. 1 (2005): 75–76.

Sutel, Seth. "It's Not All Play at Media Conference." *International Herald Tribune*, July 13, 2007. http://www.thefreelibrary.com/It%27s+not+all+play+at+media+conference-a01611373374.

Sutherland, Sharon, and Sara Swan. "The Good, the Bad, and the Justified: Moral Ambiguity in *Alias*." In *Investigating "Alias": Secrets and Spies*, edited by Stacey Abbott and Simon Brown, 119–32. London: I. B. Tauris, 2007.

Taylor, Charles. "Tom Clancy's Bogus Big-Bang Theory." Salon.com, May 31, 2002. http://www.salon.com/entertainment/movies/review/2002/05/31/sum_all_fears.

Tenet, George. *At the Center of the Storm: My Years at the CIA*. New York: HarperCollins, 2007.

———. "Does America Need the CIA?" CIA.gov, November 19, 1997. https://

www.cia.gov/news-information/speeches-testimony/1997/dci_speech_111997
.html.

"Tom Boosts CIA Image." *MX* (Melbourne), November 1, 2001.

"Two *Agency* Episodes May Not Air Due to Terrorism References." CNN.com,
November 3, 2009. http://transcripts.cnn.com/TRANSCRIPTS/0111/03/smn
.05.html.

Van der Reijden, Joël. "Summer Camp Like the Bohemian Grove, but Different."
Institute for the Study of Globalization and Covert Politics, May 27, 2005. https://
wikispooks.com/ISGP/organisations/Sun_Valley_meetings.htm.

Vinciguerra, Thomas. "Holmes Had Watson: Why Can't Bond Keep Leiter?" *New
York Times*, November 17, 2002. http://www.nytimes.com/2002/11/17/style/
cultural-studies-holmes-had-watson-why-can-t-bond-keep-leiter.html.

Weiner, Tim. *Legacy of Ashes: The History of the CIA*. New York: Doubleday, 2007.

Welch, David. "Introduction: Propaganda in Historical Perspective." In *Propaganda and Mass Persuasion: A Historical Encyclopedia, 1500 to the Present*, edited
by Nicholas John Cull, David Holbrook Culbert, and David Welch, xv–xxii.
Santa Barbara, CA: ABC-CLIO, 2002.

Wiebe, Sheldon. "*Covert Affairs*: Spy Piper Perabo Talks Up Entertaining Espionage Series!" *Eclipse Magazine*, July 12, 2010. http://www.tv.com/covert-affairs-
spy-piper-perabo-talks-up-entertaining-espionage-series!/webnews/112915
.html.

Wilford, Hugh. *The Mighty Wurlitzer: How the CIA Played America*. Cambridge,
MA: Harvard University Press, 2008.

Williams, Andrew. "Chase Brandon." *Metro*, May 25, 2005. http://www.metro
.co.uk/showbiz/interviews/180-chase-brandon.

Willing, Richard. "Spy Books Strain CIA Review Board." *USA Today*, April 30,
2007. http://www.usatoday.com/news/washington/2007-04-29-spy-books_N
.htm.

Woodhead, Leslie. "The Guardian Lecture: Dramatized Documentary." In *Why
Docudrama? Fact-Fiction on Film and TV*, edited by Alan Rosenthal, 101–10.
Carbondale: Southern Illinois University Press, 1999.

Young, Josh. "Spook Shows." *Entertainment Weekly*, September 21, 2001. http://
www.ew.com/ew/article/0,,254697,00.html.

Zakaria, Fareed. "The Failures That Led to Sept. 11." *Washington Post*, January
15, 2002. http://pqasb.pqarchiver.com/washingtonpost/access/99641039.html
?FMT=ABS&FMTS=ABS:FT&date=Jan+15,+2002&author=Fareed+Zakaria
&pub=The+Washington+Post&edition=&startpage=A.19&desc=The+Fail
ures+That+Led+To+Sept.+11.

Index